LOVE AND THE NOVEL

LOVE AND THE NOVEL

LIFE AFTER READING

CHRISTINA LUPTON

P

PROFILE BOOKS

First published in Great Britain in 2022 by
Profile Books Ltd
29 Cloth Fair
London
ECIA 7JQ
www.profilebooks.com

1 3 5 7 9 10 8 6 4 2

Typeset in Garamond by MacGuru Ltd
Printed and bound in Great Britain by Clays Ltd, Elcograf S.p.A.

A CIP catalogue record for this book is available from the British Library.

ISBN 978 1 78816 647 8
eISBN 978 1 78283 766 4

CONTENTS

CHAPTER ONE

THE ORIGINALITY OF LOVE

In November 2018 I sat at the side of an indoor pool while my son Rohan took his swimming class. It was already dark, the way it gets on winter afternoons in Denmark. The sports centre was stoked with artificial warmth and light, and the sound of children's voices filled the glassy space. Rohan dived for weighted plastic in a squall of other eight-year-olds. A swimming teacher stood and cast rings for them, one by one, into the water – a green one to the right, a blue one to the left, the look on his face of someone feeding ducks in a pond. My coat and hat were spread beside me on the slatted bench and I'd taken a novel from my bag. I see myself now at a distance, as if looking back into that terrarium of human life: a woman watching her child plumb the depths of the pool. From the outside, she seems to have been many places and read many books. Less visible are the thoughts of the love affair, just started, trumpeting silently through her head and out into the chlorinated air.

It seems unlikely that falling in love could do much to a life as well populated and extended as mine was then. Hans and I had been together for decades. We lived in a nice part of Copenhagen, in a building by a canal lined with blue and pink houses and weekend sailing boats. Hans had renovated the flat, carved out a kitchen from an old beer cellar and decorated rooms for the kids. I had a job at a university in England and commuted most weeks of the term between our home and London, teaching literature classes prepped on the plane to well-read students. When I wasn't travelling, my days were filled with smaller routines. I biked around the city and met friends for coffee. I read bedtime stories, spent weekends at the summerhouse in Sweden, cooked meals, spoke at conferences, researched life in England in the eighteenth century. The book on my lap that day at the pool was *Pride and Prejudice*, carried in my bag because I'd agreed to produce by the end of the year an introduction for a new edition of the novel.

In taking on the project, I'd said I would describe the different kinds of love represented by Austen: between sisters, and between friends; love that is just lust; love that connects parents and children, even when they seem not to like each other much. More precisely, I wanted to explain the case Austen makes for reconciling romantic and heartfelt love with the kinds of socially productive marriage promoted in the early nineteenth century. At the time when Austen wrote there were plenty of reasons to get married, but little basis for believing in romantic and conjugal life as the same thing. It remained rare in her short lifetime to think that one had to fall in love with the person one married, or to assume that one could marry the person one loved. Children were cared for, obviously, but they were also routinely sent away to wet nurses or to school, or out early to work. The family at the centre of so many novels wasn't yet there as the emotional crux it seems now. As I watched Rohan swim, my finger marked the part of the story when Elizabeth wanders around Darcy's estate, believing that he's away from home. She's already refused his first proposal of marriage, but he's about to reappear in her life as someone she can't resist. It's a famous turning point in a book so familiar to me that I hardly needed to read the words again. Yet the connection between what Austen writes and what love really is, or was, seemed looser to me than it ever had.

In all these decades of teaching and writing about literature, one thing I've learned is that novels aren't blueprints for living; their stories do not bleed straight into our brains; they don't reveal truthfully what we think, or what we do with our bodies. The writer's job is not, as the poet Elizabeth Bishop once warned her friend Robert Lowell, to *tell what we're really like in 1972*. Jane Austen also wasn't writing to tell what love was like in 1810. If historians of the future dig up our libraries, the books we've written – those old ones we've kept reading and translating and turning into television shows – I hope they won't say, *Ah, that is how they were, that is how they loved back then*. I'm not sure we should read the fictions of any time that way, by joining too closely the dots between the novels we read and the things we do, the people we are. Knowing that I was born in the 1970s in a commune in London, or that I studied in the 1990s, working my way into a job as a literature professor during those years of queer and feminist debate, or that this story starts with me being unfaithful to a husband I loved, tells you a lot. But none of that puts me easily in the novels I have read or explains how reading them supported the new shape my life was taking.

A friend came to Copenhagen once with a copy of Elizabeth Hardwick's *Sleepless Nights* for me in her bag. Like gifts she'd brought before, it was perfectly chosen. The intricate prose kept me awake at night, puzzling out the point of view and admiring the author. Hardwick wrote her novel late in the 1970s, just after her divorce from Lowell, that poet prone to telling it all. At the point Hardwick and Lowell divorced, they had a teenage daughter, an apartment in Manhattan and an impressive group of literary friends. Looking back at her life from that vantage point, Hardwick describes in *Sleepless Nights* some places she has been. At one point she offers a succinct account of it all:

> Tickets, migration, worries, property, debts, changes of name and changes back once more: these came about from reading many books. So, from Kentucky to New York, to Boston, to Maine, to Europe, carried along on a river of paragraphs and chapters, or blank verse, of little books translated from the Polish, large books from the Russian – all consumed in a sedentary sleeplessness.

This, she says, is the true though insufficient explanation of her life. The books she's read are coordinates, but they are not a map. With reading as her mode of travel, she has been a passenger without destination, a woman finding her way, balancing her wishes against the grain of other narratives.

Hardwick's description of her life came back to me as I thought about *Pride and Prejudice*. In the essay I wrote on the novel during that long winter of 2018, I argued that Austen's emphasis on individual feelings is the key to the novel's innovative representation of love. If we want to understand why novels have mattered so much in the history of emotion, it's not enough to think of the marriages and trysts they describe. We must think of the whole experience of reading fiction as a lesson in having and discovering personal feelings, almost regardless of what one does with them, or how they relate to society's standards for living well. Before the middle of the 1700s, which is when people really began to buy novels for the first time, there were plenty of texts explaining what to feel: sermons, pornography, romance, travel narratives, satires, tragic plays. But none of them set as much store by individual response as the novel. Reading them didn't involve a journey of the kind Hardwick describes, *carried along on a river of paragraphs*, prone to divergence from any route mapped out in advance.

Individual romantic love and the novel emerged together in the eighteenth century, partook from the outset of each other's values, became testing grounds at the same time for the ideal of original selfhood. The lover who followed her heart would not be swayed in the end by what her parents or her religion told her. This individual celebrated and cultivated by the novel was able to feel for herself, to make rational choices, to defy rules, to read her own way through a story. It was for her sake – and not simply in the name of the partnerships and profits they represented – that novels helped drive arranged marriage and orthodox religion into decline. Unlike the sermons and conduct books that kept on circulating alongside them, novels weren't simple prescriptions for how to live. Even *Pride and Prejudice*, which ultimately reconciles that new level of feeling with a larger sense of social responsibility, was a primer in the logic of heartfelt choice.

This explains why novel-reading was also associated in those early decades of its existence with the incitement of rebellion and change. A daughter who read novels was more likely to insist on choosing for herself than one who didn't. Fiction built in this larger sense on all Enlightenment thinking. Don't trust your teachers, or your doctors, or your priests. The most radical questions that philosophers and politicians were asking in the late 1700s required members of the public to think, as well as feel, for themselves. Shouldn't all laws be put to the test of individual belief? Should one really obey a king? What disqualified enslaved people and women from having the rights of free men? Shouldn't I be allowed to change my mind? *To love at fifty someone different from the one I loved in my youth?*

For the famous radicals of Austen's time, novels helped show that feelings could be a force for good, a way of driving the machinery of change forward. Jean-Jacques Rousseau, Johann Wolfgang von Goethe, Thomas Paine, William Godwin and Mary Wollstonecraft: all of them argued in various ways for a new world that would be built on true emotion. They claimed that children might be better brought up away from the corruption of polite society; that parents and rulers should earn and not simply claim these children's affection; that stereotypes of women as passive and vulnerable were wrong; that no man should command respect automatically. *I love my man as my fellow*, argues Wollstonecraft, *but his sceptre, real, or usurped, extends not to me, unless the reason of an individual demands my homage; and even then the submission is to reason, and not to man.*

Those writers criticised the old romances and sentimental stereotypes, fantasies of women submissive to convention and seduction. They wrote novels encouraging personal relations needing renewal and reason, able at their best to cut through the hypocrisy of habit, of tradition, of patriarchy.

Yet there were writers on the other side of that political divide who tried to enlist love's conservative force as something oriented towards community and tradition. Edmund Burke wrote about the French Revolution, criticising the violence of the people against their monarch, showing what was lost when individuals began to question the authorities they were meant to look up to. Surely, he insists in his *Reflections on the Revolution in France* (1790), the feelings of loyalty towards one's king and country should not be put to the test. He praises love of social hierarchy, admonishing the French for approaching this emotion as a matter for philosophy. Love belongs, he exhorts, to the youthful realm of *grace* and *manners*, not to the realm of philosophical reflection. Conservatism, just like radicalism, should be felt, not thought through. The kind of individual feelings rallied by fiction could also be directed towards monarchs, nations, conventions; the kinds of feelings that people should nurture are those supporting the family, the sovereign, the child. For Burke, it was inappropriate of the loyal subject or wife to think too hard about whom she loved.

Pride and Prejudice was written and rewritten at the fulcrum of those debates, which were sharp in my mind those last months of 2018, when my job was to write about novels, to teach them, and also to decide how to live the next part of my life. We were long past the age of Romantic revolt

when lovers' feelings might help overturn a whole conservative regime. My own dilemmas had little in common with
Elizabeth Bennet's. No one had expected me to marry. The
cohesion of society did not depend upon my family unit.
Yet my questions about what passionate love counts for,
about what might make it original and true and when one
could legitimately be guided by it, weren't so different from
the ones Austen tried to answer. *Pride and Prejudice* makes
the case for love being discovered and felt by an individual
without being too scripted or coerced. Elizabeth cannot fall
in love with Darcy as she does, in her own terms, without
going through all the difficult stages of doubt and reason-
ing that result in her that hard-won, crystalline conviction
that he is right for her. At the same time the partnership that
Elizabeth chooses for herself is the one her small-minded
mother would have chosen for her. Nothing about the relation between Elizabeth and Darcy upsets the conventions
governing class and gender and heterosexuality. The lovers
whose happiness is promoted make independent choices,
based on their own feelings. But the choices they make
are the ones conservative society inclines to. The fact that
Austen's protagonists think and suffer and consider as they
love is part of a more general compromise brokered in her
fiction, between feeling as something true for the individual,
and love as something that requires ethical deliberation and
community sanction.

I went into my love affair with Austen in my pocket,
thinking of her in these terms as the architect of the romance
plot compatible both with original feeling *and* a larger social
order. The happily-ever-after love that her characters are

promised comes to those who wait and judge, not to those who desire too much or act too recklessly. Elizabeth makes it a point of pride that she has never gone as far as to fall in love with the rakish Wickham. Lydia, Elizabeth's younger sister, who does fall in love and elope with him, will never be happy. Real love is a reward for getting to the end of the story with one's individual feelings vindicated and one's moral integrity still intact. To love and to read radically *and* reasonably, Austen suggests, will yield new kinds of truth in reward. But to love too lustily or too sentimentally is to fall for convention, to abandon a reasonable course of action for something more ephemeral. As a reader of fiction, one prepares for love to count for everything, as well as to foresee and avoid the dangers of cliché, genre, sentiment. In twenty-first-century terms, falling as deeply as I had for another woman in the middle of my life might be radical or newly conventional; it might be just desire, or it might be truth.

Shortly before that day at the Danish pool I'd been at the British Library, studying letters from the 1790s and attending a conference at Birkbeck called 'New Worlds of the Novel'. Shannon, a fellow critic I knew by reputation but had never met, was there too. We spent consecutive evenings drinking at the bar of the hotel where the speakers were staying. Under dim lights we perched on stools between mirrored columns and tore at our beer mats in excitement over conversation that was unfathomably good. On the last day, once the organisers had summed things up by telling us that the novel was alive and well, Shannon and I broke away from the group and took a bus up to Hampstead Heath. In the open fields, breathing clouds of condensation, telling stories of our families, of being young in Kentucky and in Sussex, we took a path that led higher out of the city, leaving London looking grey and jagged in the distance and bringing us out in a far corner of Highgate.

From there we could go to the Freud Museum, I said. I liked the ordinariness of that place, it being both a museum and a house. It was something I could show an American in London, the city of my birth and a place where I had spent significant happy patches of my itinerant life. We went to the museum late and lingered as closing time approached in the rooms stacked with the tapestries and totems Freud had brought from Vienna, the famous couch behind tasselled ropes, the doors opening onto the garden. This was where Freud died and where his family went on living without him. Placards detailed their immigration to London, the epiphanies of Freud's career. The self is a honeycomb of secrets shaped by desires we may not even know we have. Shannon and I were both steeped in that argument. But it's hard, when thrilling to the nape of a neck, to fathom the idea that there could be anything deeper than what one most obviously feels. Waiting for a taxi to take us back to the hotel, leaning against Freud's garden wall in a state of ineffable happiness, I felt only desire. A psychoanalytic reading might reveal those rose bushes bedded down and barren of fruit as omens of a long winter to come, but I saw nothing but the beauty of their stubbly selves.

Long before Freud discovered the unconscious, novelists invented characters who had difficulty recognising their own feelings. In some sense, fictional selves became realistic at the point where they wanted things they could not name. This is the gist of one of the earliest modern love stories, Madame de Lafayette's *The Princesse de Clèves*, the first text on the 'Love and the Novel' course I sometimes taught. More fairy tale than fully-fledged novel, the late seventeenth-century story reckons differently from *Pride and Prejudice* with the new psychology of love. The princess is very young and beautiful, and marries as she should – a man she respects and of whom her mother approves. Her husband loves her excessively, more like a mistress than a wife. But the love he wants from her exceeds by far what wives at the time are encouraged to feel. The demure princess does not understand what she is being accused of withholding. What can be missing from this marriage in which she happily complies? Then a young duke arrives in the French court and the princess dances with him. The electric current flowing between them makes the whole court murmur.

The married princess is the last in this scenario to realise what is happening. It is only when she hears a rumour that the duke has taken a lover that she discovers feelings for him that she hasn't dared confess to herself. Love dawns on her as a sudden and unwelcome truth. At the point where she sees she is capable of the love that her husband wants from her, her feelings are directed firmly towards another. Overcome with shame at not being able to control her own heart, the princess is distraught. The breaching of the wall between her conscious and unconscious mind is painful. She wants to tell her husband everything, but she feels betrayed by a desire that cannot possibly be reconciled with the world. For the rest of the novel she tries desperately to regain control over a story too easily legible to those around her as sex and scandal.

There's no doubt that Lafayette recognises the radical power of desire to upend other kinds of convention. Yet she, like Austen, does not see it offering women a simple form of liberation. The princess's escape from one story – of court etiquette and arranged marriage – writes her into another one just as scripted, of her own lust. She feels as fully deprived of her volition as a lover as she did as a wife. While she is tempted to reject the constraints of marriage, the princess would not be freer if she did. She and the duke have already become characters in a romance that people are reading. Society tells them what they want, as well as what they are not allowed. Socially defined answers to the question of the princess's desire anticipate Freud's claims for the power of the subconscious. The only way out of the impasse, the princess decides, is to avoid love all together. When her husband dies, she goes to a monastery rather than into the arms of the Duke of Nemours.

Today's students tend to resent the idea of a self not in charge of its feelings. The emphasis on the princess being the last to know what she really wants reads strangely in this climate of consent. The next novel on that 'Love and the Novel' syllabus, Samuel Richardson's *Pamela*, has also become harder to read with students than it used to be. Written almost a century after *The Princesse de Clèves*, this English novel of letters describes the romance between a young aristocrat and his mother's servant. On the face of things, it's a happier story for its lovers: despite the scandal of their alliance, Pamela and Mr B end up married. But Pamela's equivocations of agency make it hard for twenty-first-century students to see her story as radical. Richardson was a middle-class and middle-aged publisher when he invented his famous character. Ostensibly he started ventriloquising his girl heroine while he was meant to be writing a book of letter templates for novice writers to imitate. His blow-by-blow account of Pamela's attempts to avoid the sexual advances of Mr B is steamy and full of near-misses. The novel was a media sensation, well read and debated, a scandal in its own time. Pamela's innocence seems implausible, the scenes of almost-rape that she describes more obviously titillating than the framing of it all as morality tale admits, and the idea of love as an avenue of upward mobility for beautiful young women mildly offensive.

Like the princess, Pamela is also less known to herself than to a wider community of onlookers. She has several chances to escape Mr B's hold on her. But she stays in his house to finish a waistcoat she is embroidering for him, then because she misconstrues the cows in the field outside the house as bulls. The longer this goes on, the more likely it begins to seem that she wants him more than she admits in her letters. Readers can feel forced to countenance what seem today like scenes of harassment, to see Pamela inviting the attention – perhaps even the sex – on offer. The realist script, given to us as the letters she writes to her parents, asks to be read between the lines. Despite what she says, it becomes clear how much she desires Mr B. It also becomes difficult for a good twenty-first-century feminist to know how to interpret this.

In the middle of the eighteenth century satires recast Pamela as a knowing pretender, more designing of marriage than Richardson allows. Today, the emphasis falls on her right to say no. The age of Byronic heroes who intuit what women really want, or of women who can't help but fall for them, is over. The Freudian idea of unconscious desire is still with us, but it is harder now to reconcile with a robust idea of women's choice. Elizabeth wins fans for refusing Darcy the first time he proposes to her, even if we suspect that she likes him more than she knows. When she ends up wandering around his estate as a tourist, Austen's godlike hand, not Elizabeth's sublimated desire, seems to be directing things. Yet it's clear that the process of Elizabeth falling in love with Darcy involves – just as clearly as that of Pamela coming to love Mr B – a slow growth in her own awareness of what a community of readers already know she wants. Darcy and Elizabeth are revealed to us as a perfect match for each other long before they discover this themselves. Their love may be radical, but we have given them permission to feel it.

I met Shannon when I had already been talking for decades with students about sex and marriage, the agency of lovers who defy convention; teaching classes circling this problem of where real originality lies, of whether the union of man and wife can ever be anything but a violent norm, of whether love is a story worth telling at all. In the luxurious classrooms of Williams College; at the University of Michigan, where my students padded across the quadrangles in their puffy coats and fur boots; back in England, teaching the British novels I'd grown up reading in Australia – in every one of these settings I had led groups undecided on whether love sits deep within the individual or whether it's merely a script inserting us into a world already decided. To me, the princess's dilemma still seemed unsolved: that puzzle of whether it's worse to submit to desires you cannot fathom or to follow the rules imposed from the outside. Freudian logic doesn't deliver you from social coercion. If I write about travelling back with Shannon through London from the Freud Museum, the winter sunset streaking the chemically tinted sky, our gloved hands touching on the back seat of the taxi, do you already know what should happen? When we come to the hotel and stand in the mirrored lobby the last night before I am due to fly back to my family, you may know better than I did at the time which way to turn.

After that night in London, everything changed. But on the surface of things, my life stayed the same. Shannon flew home to the US and I went back to marking student papers and living in my home by the canal with Hans and Rohan and Marie. I told Hans that I'd fallen in love with someone else, but that seemed to overstate the reality. For the rest of the winter it was my reading and my letter-writing that swivelled towards Shannon. Postponing my work on Austen each morning when everyone left the house, I called up the things she had written online. There's a special kind of pleasure that comes from listening, across the distance of print, to a voice that has just breathed endearments into your ear. After reading proofs of William Godwin's essays at the time they were living down the road from each other, Mary Wollstonecraft wrote of *sensations, that have been clustering round my heart, as I read this morning – reminding myself, every now and then, that the writer loved me.* Shannon's fine lines of argument filled me with the same kind of admiration two centuries later, had me wondering what it would be like to hear them from her naked beside me.

When I finished reading her writing, I began reading the novels she wrote about in her work. I went back to the early twentieth-century fictions by American authors I'd studied in graduate school in the US: descriptions of muddy banks, Native burial mounds, sparsely populated piny coastlines. In those novels, nature is a force unsettling the way people live in towns, in couples, in houses. The more authentic characters are the lonely ones, people on horseback or in little boats between islands, the queer ones whose community seems to lie in the future or the past. Spinsters and misfits meet up on occasion, their desires pent up so far below the surface that whole lives are locked for ever in impossible lust. Herbs and fir, and no one watching. *Do you really like these novels?* I asked Shannon in one of the long emails I wrote every day, doubting that she was in fact akin to their characters. When I first read Willa Cather and Sarah Orne Jewett in my twenties, I'd been impatient with all that loneliness and pushed back against their stories, identifying myself as the child of European collectives, impervious to such New World statelessness and individualism.

But as the Christmas of 2018 loomed, I felt more alone than I'd been for a long time. I had to finish my essay on *Pride and Prejudice*. I had to find out, as I explained to Hans, *what this feeling was, if it was anything at all.* I couldn't do that while going to gatherings in Copenhagen, where people snipped away happily at intricate paper Christmas decorations and made delicate cardamom cookies. I seemed always to be walking down along the icy cobbled street for a stolen minute on the phone with Shannon, or fighting with Rohan about too many hours of *Minecraft*. I couldn't do it all under the teenage eyes of Marie, asking me what was wrong; or in the office of the therapist whom Hans had enlisted to help us talk things through. In an effort to give me space, Hans drove me out to a small cabin in the south of Sweden that his parents had helped him buy. We slipped across the bridges, supplies of firewood and canned food in the car and Leonard Cohen songs playing to hide the silence, and Hans drove off again before dark, back home to the kids.

The lake beside the cabin was frozen just enough to walk on, and I crossed it between sessions of reading and writing and dreaming of limbs and tongues. The lines of my footprints intersected with the tracks of birds, whimsical in their circles and figures of eight on the ice. I thought the firm surface might break and swallow me up, or that I might simply keep walking into the darkness of the forest. But that would have meant missing the emails I downloaded slowly each day onto my offline computer, toggled to Shannon's through a phone signal too weak to carry sound. I walked to places where huge mushrooms ballooned to life in autumn and small flowers pricked the moss in spring; to places I had been with Hans and the kids and friends, and in which I had imagined our future. I sat so long hoping to see deer that my hands numbed and the fire had burned out when I got back to the cabin. The next morning I had a fever and brought my books and notepads into bed.

In the days of my sickness, Shannon and I read Thomas Mann's *The Magic Mountain* in tandem. She'd taken her copy of the novel on holiday with her to a hotel in the Caribbean while I'd taken mine to Sweden. The only love story in *The Magic Mountain*, which is set almost entirely in a Swiss sanatorium, is obsessive and risible. Castorp waits in a state of luxurious incarceration for Clawdia, who comes and goes annually as a way to manage her own marriage. At the high point of his obsession, Castorp praises a portrait the doctor has made of her, commenting on every pore of her painted skin. Oh, the joy when he procures an X-ray taken of her heart, using a new technology that enters the human body with magic fingers. The single night the two spend together is carefully concealed in Mann's narrative, almost skipped over. But whole pages are dedicated to Castorp rising from the dining table to rearrange a curtain so that the sun doesn't shine on Clawdia's face. The prose itself gets slowed down by his drippy state of devotion. His deep attention to Clawdia justifies and colours Mann's description of everything else.

Shannon wrote in her letters to me of reading *The Magic Mountain* by a hotel pool. Stoned and sunburnt, she retold Castorp's fantasies of the female form back to me – Clawdia beamed at galaxy-size across the sky, the inner flesh of her arms exposed as she leans down to embrace Castorp from the sky. I stoked the fire and ate chickpeas and chocolate and worked on the footnotes for *Pride and Prejudice*, trying to focus on the details of shoes and sandwiches in the 1810s. The introductory essay was done. Writing it had allowed me to articulate something I really believed about novel-reading, which is that it can be a model for love that is grounded in intellection and open to reconsideration. Loving as Elizabeth does need not involve finding one's own Darcy: it may simply be a matter of falling for a novel as good as *Pride and*

Prejudice, a narrator as good as Austen's. Working this argument out, though, had not helped me decide what to do about my own affair, or what exactly to say to Hans back in Copenhagen.

Instead of reaching any conclusions, I read the chapters of *The Magic Mountain* that Shannon invoked, with my own body in play. I was still coughing like the patients at the sanatorium as I lay propped beside the fire. At night, my fever rose and the sounds of animals boomed in my brain. The barking of deer and the sounds of ice shifting felt like sighs coming from my lungs. I missed Hans and the kids, wondered what they were all doing on those long winter nights. On the first day of 2019 a letter from Shannon arrived. She described reading *The Magic Mountain* on a bus crossing the island to the airport, looking up to see the parties of the people who lived there still going in the tropical dawn. Our settings were so far apart but I felt her next to me, the pages of the novel like a filament of joy between us. It was hopeless to say I wouldn't see her.

In February I flew to New York. There was a long-planned conference in my calendar, but Hans and I now viewed the trip as a dangerous point of reckoning. In our therapy sessions we kept talking about our relationship, but to me, that felt like looking backwards. Does there have to be something wrong with one life for another to become more desirable? I could only think in very specific terms about the trip to come. The plane landed in an unseasonal snowstorm and sat banked in a long queue on the runway for hours. I could feel Shannon in the terminal, her car out there somewhere in the carpet of Newark's car parks, but my phone wasn't working. Instead of calling, I finished Patricia Highsmith's *The Price of Salt*, which I had begun back in Copenhagen. The novel is about a love affair between women, but I was not reading to find out about that. I was so invested in the singularity of my love that I couldn't imagine researching it. What I liked was the way the affair on the page felt like a thing one could get hold of and slow down. In the case of *The Price of Salt*, everything except the ending had already been revealed to me. The friend who'd told me the plot had not given that away. The romance starts in the toy section of a department store, where Therese is working as a sales assistant. Carol, older and beautiful, comes in to buy a Christmas present for her daughter and, when Therese sees her, everything else stops. It takes for ever for Carol to reach the counter.

In 1952, when the novel was published, many things stood in the way of that relationship, which is slow to start and seems unlikely to flourish. Carol, just separated from her husband and fresh from a love affair with her friend Abby, is legally vulnerable to her husband's claims to custody of their daughter. Yet in the second part of the novel, Carol gets Therese recklessly into her car and they drive, almost in a dream, out across America. They become lovers on their journey, plotting their route, whirling from motel to motel, washing up in small towns each afternoon. The excessive movement gives the story traction, and it speeds up when the couple find themselves followed by a detective that Carol's husband has hired to expose them. But desire intercepts their progress, slowing down the road trip dramatically when the women end up looking at each other across a table or lying beside each other, eating an orange or drinking milk. Even when the chase is at its height, Carol and Therese's nights are unhurried. Highsmith registers the small details of Carol's hairbrush, a hotel fixture; sex is the element into which they retreat at night.

Reading this novel on that landlocked plane, its different currents of movement and stillness ran through me. I remembered the hyperbolic energies of the journeys taken with Hans over the years, the moves between London and New York and Copenhagen, along the roads through Sweden and Germany. There on the runway that movement that had kept me criss-crossing the Atlantic for so long felt halted in some dramatic way. Tired and fallen out of time, my body became one of those in *The Magic Mountain* coddled in blankets, ruffled by the winds of death and joy. One ten-minute snowstorm might last a lifetime. Perhaps desire was a form of energy more sustainable than jet fuel, but it no longer seemed like one that would get me somewhere. Instead, it seemed to bypass all the novel's native forms of progress, the whole world of narrative. If only Therese and Carol could lie still long enough that the movement driving their century of expansion, disaster, disillusion and reproduction would wind down and leave them to occupy the world in their own terms. Falling in love seemed like an eddy in time, an opportunity to opt out of the imperative to be always doing and moving and making. How ironic that novelists – some of the greatest poets of love – should have been obliged formally to keep characters on the move, shackled to plot.

Those months in Copenhagen I had resisted the feeling of being in a story of the kind that could ever be told in a novel. It didn't have to be going anywhere; didn't have to be a tragic affair or a romance. Yet, strapped to my plane seat, I was also glued to that novel. In the last pages of *The Price of Salt*, Carol leaves Therese and goes back to New York to fight for custody of her daughter. She loses, but the two meet again and, on an evening full of possibility, Carol invites Therese to come and live with her. Therese says yes. The mother and child getting parted is hard to fathom, but the lovers being together trumps the loss. When I reached the final page, gratitude towards Highsmith for that ending overcame me. She had published the novel pseudonymously and never really found its happiness herself. To read *The Price of Salt* seventy years later as a benediction of my own prospects was surely to read it badly. And yet the book made me feel that a happy ending was already at hand, unfolded and there waiting for me to walk into it.

On the runway little vehicles were blinking, reversing, charging forward again, in small efforts to get things moving. The guy next to me was playing *Angry Birds* on his phone. *Could I use it to make a call?* Shannon sounded far away, for someone standing right there in a building visible in the distance. I told her we were still stuck on the runway. She had thought so, said it didn't matter, said she would wait.

CHAPTER TWO

THE ROMANCE OF YOUTH

I met Hans in 1994 when I was twenty-three. I had read a lot of novels by then, but I was convinced that traditional romance of the getting-married kind should be avoided. From my vantage point, people who fell in love were irrational, prone to mistakes and probable traitors to the feminist cause. An older friend had told me playfully that she thought all the states associated with absolute devotion – to a sick infant, or a dying parent, or a new lover – were brought on by mind-altering degrees of sleeplessness. I liked that line of conjecture and offered it up drunkenly at parties so that people knew I wasn't looking for any relationship that would keep me too much awake.

Elizabeth Hardwick applied a similarly sober logic to Robert Lowell's behaviour when he announced that he was leaving her for Caroline Blackwood. Hardwick had seen Lowell through several spells of infatuation during their marriage, and Blackwood, an English socialite with kitten-ish ways, was a hard rival for a seasoned literary critic to take seriously. In breaking up with her to join Blackwood and her three daughters in the English countryside, Lowell seemed to Hardwick to have entered a new period of mental disarray, unseemly mania. Emboldened and morose by turn, writing long poems about his feelings, Lowell insisted in letters to Hardwick that his passion for Caroline was the real thing, just as true as anything that had ever happened between them. But Hardwick was sceptical. This comes out in their published correspondence, not in *Sleepless Nights*, which touches only in passing on Hardwick's relations with men. Despite her own sleeplessness, and her very fully developed sensitivities to fiction, Hardwick seemed by her fifties to have outgrown romantic love.

My own scepticism about love has flown in the reverse direction. That gullible reader I was of Shannon's words, drunk with love in my late forties, would have seemed immature to my twenty-three-year-old self. As the child of adults keen to rewrite the rules, I had grasped early the idea that novels were not rules to be followed. In 1974, when I was three, my parents took me and my younger brother to Australia. Leaving London for a freer, wilder world, they joined close friends they had lived with in a commune. In Adelaide, a city spreading out thinly on either side of a muddy river, they became part of a bigger community of people interested in art and folk music. The new friends they made were committed to public housing and food co-ops and living collectively on the land. My youngest brother was born in 1977, two years before my parents separated and began a season of tumultuous love affairs and experiments in counter-culture that I watched with curiosity and suspicion.

Through all those years I read novels from libraries and found on shelves at home. Most of the settings I read about were unlike the real ones I lived in. There were no otters or hedgehogs or snowmen in South Australia, no country mansions to shelter children displaced by a great war, no boarding schools, no extended family gatherings. It was evident to me from the start that however truly novels spoke, their truths were unverifiable. Perhaps they told of lovers who found each other in the end, made domestic concord the descant to every other grief that children faced, but they offered no proof life was like that. All the things I confirmed later as a critic of literature, about language being a way to impose a shape upon the world rather than a description of its contours, started for me in those early days of hungry, out-of-place reading.

At nine, I opened for the first time a novel that lined up better than most with the world around me. Helen Garner's *Monkey Grip* is a daring first-person narrative, telling without narcissism or rancour of life in the shared houses of inner Melbourne in the late 1970s. Although I was too young to understand it when I took it from my father's bedside table, I hoovered it into my brain as evidence that fiction might illuminate what real people did. Garner's setting was a city of sun and friendly chaos, and drugs and slow, passionate sex. Just like my mother, the narrator, Nora, spent her time on group camping trips, cycling to the public pool in the heat, renovating old houses, scraping by financially. The story follows Nora's infatuation with the blue-eyed junkie Javo, and her care for her daughter, Grace.

I read *Monkey Grip* in a single afternoon while my father sat in a director's chair on the patio, drinking white wine from a two-litre box that he kept in his empty fridge. He was convivial and good-humoured in those days, but left us mostly to entertain ourselves. Dry spider ferns hung from the doorways of his rented house in macramé baskets, with clay beads threaded onto jute in crafty twists. For long weeks during the summer holidays my brothers and I lay around on the linoleum floor, sucking popsicles and waiting for something to happen. Joni Mitchell and John Denver played on the record player, the soundtrack from the 1973 movie *Sunshine* interweaving with the voice of a young mother dying from cancer, explaining how much she misses being able to make love as she used to. Sometimes a girlfriend came to visit my father and we'd all go out to eat pizza, or my brothers and I would get bored of their flirtations and drift off to sleep. *Monkey Grip*, which hinges on the obsessive affair between Nora and Javo, includes many scenes in which Nora waits helplessly for Javo to come to her bed. The novel helped me diagnose my father's single life as being shot through with a similar kind of malaise and addiction.

Around that same time, my mother and a friend of hers took us to picnic at a small waterfall outside the city. When we arrived, there was a dead sheep floating in the pool at the base of the falls and we ended up playing in the shade of the gum-nutty riverbank above the rapids. We ate from a Tupperware box of sandwiches yeasty with home-made bread. Two young men came and sat along the bank, throwing sticks into the water for their dog, looking over to make sure my mother and her friend were watching. The dog went out further each time, eventually getting carried along towards the point where the water sloped down into the falls. My mother jumped up when the men started calling the dog's name. Dropping her sandwich, stripping off her top and denim shorts, she swam into the river, pale and slight and dark-haired. When she brought the dog back in her arms out of the brown rapids, hair sprouted from the seams of her torn cotton underwear. The men thanked her while she stood topless and fine in the sun, then asked her if she was free later for a beer.

My mother's life converged with *Monkey Grip* even more poignantly than my father's. The novel confirmed my view of adults crying, or flirting, or leaving on a motorbike in the middle of the night while drunk on sexy love. A fey man with John Lennon glasses, who didn't speak much and built pantomime sets out of wood, came to see my mother when we were meant to be sleeping. Another with long, waxy hair and outreaching hands worked with her in the food co-op, feeling her up among the bins of dates and bran. The indoor pool down the road hosted nude swimming evenings where my mother took us on winter nights. After slow laps of breaststroke in the dimmed downlight of the main hall, people lingered to eat dried fruit and wholemeal cake in the yoga room. Wet skin and cake crumbs, naked bodies chatting and flirting, falling in love. The man my mother chose to live with in the end did not like the naked swimming nights. With Garner's help, I saw it all from a child's-eye perspective as one undulating human landscape, a sticky place of slow pleasure and possibility.

When I was thirteen my mother moved to a country town in a region of vineyards and almond orchards. She and her new partner borrowed money on a government scheme for low-income people and bought a small piece of land. Slowly they began to build a house of mud-bricks and recycled timber.

I was enrolled in the high school nearby, where classes were held in transportable buildings and big paddocks and dusty sports fields. I walked to school along a road lined with gum trees and criss-crossed by swooping magpies. The beach was five miles away, which meant the kids that I met were all interested in cars. My stepsisters, who came from their mother's house in the city on the weekends, read teen magazines and stole nail polish from the town chemist. By the time I was fourteen I was skipping classes, lying on my bed or beside the creek across from the school, working my way along my mother's bookshelves.

I breezed through *Madame Bovary* in that setting, stomach down on the bed in the room I shared with my brothers. Caught up in Gustave Flaubert's story, I missed the irony of Emma and me being readers whose choice of novels made life harder in the worlds we lived in. But I took Flaubert's warning against romance to heart. Emma, wife of the local doctor and mother of a young child, pines for the luxury and drama of the fictional characters she reads about. When Rodolphe, a local landowner, seduces her, a bridge opens up between her world and theirs. She feels herself lifted out of the mud, the small-town routines. The first time she and Rodolphe make love, outdoors, as their horses graze beside them, the air becomes a lofty blue. She looks back at her ordinary existence through the clouds. Her rapture doesn't last. The crescendo of that affair subsides, and of her next one, and she retreats, sheepish and impoverished, to her husband and her daughter and an early death.

But my literary taste was mostly not for Romance. I gravitated in my teens towards what I only now know to call modernist literature, novels of alienation rather than union. On my mother's shelves I found Carson McCullers, Somerset Maugham, Muriel Spark, E. M. Forster, D. H. Lawrence, Janet Frame and Thomas Hardy and could get through one of their works for every day I didn't go to school. My mother was working constantly in those days to earn money for building the house – harvesting fruit, cleaning houses, getting up early to sort and deliver the mail, moulding mudbricks in the afternoon. If I ever found her with a book, it had fallen from her hand in sleep. But I read novels that she had collected late at night, and then hunted down at the council library others by any author I liked. Homing in on early twentieth-century texts, I skipped over nineteenth-century fictions written to map out and render legible a sprawling social system. Modernists broke with that project of making sense of the world, aligning desire with existing codes of morality. To me, they showed instead how rich the unhappy self could be.

One morning I skipped my home-economics class and took Carson McCullers's *The Member of the Wedding* to a shady spot by the creek. The 1946 novel follows twelve-year-old Frankie, *an unjoined person* killing time during a small-town summer in the American South. Over the course of a few weeks she watches preparations for her older brother's wedding to a girl who seems, from a distance, to be an icon of style and good luck. Frankie is suspended between the shared beds of her childhood and the fantasy of the ones she will lie in with a lover when she becomes an adult; between days that she spends chatting with the household help and the allure and horror of the sex on offer with the older men in the town. She observes the engaged couple at a distance, deep in her own state of agitation and arousal, fixating on the idea that they might carry her away with them, swoop her into the space of their shared interiority and out of the town.

From Frankie's perspective, I could see how desirable mobility was. I could also see that sex might be a way to spin narrative gold from the flax of country-town existence. In my own way I experimented recklessly in getting the boys at school to notice me. In the back of cars, wine-cooler squirted straight into the mouth. *I'll give you more to drink if you show me your tits. You can suck me off, if you like.* Frankie goes to a hotel room with a grown man. But my heavily moustached English teacher only ever gave me Jack Kerouac's novels in return for the suggestive notes I sent him. I wrote as well to a boy in Sydney whose address I'd found in the pen-pal section of a magazine. His letters to me came full of badly drawn fantasies of what he would do to me if we were together, lined paper sprayed with cheap aftershave and sprouting loose cuttings of pubic hair.

My mother's books promised more in their materiality than romance. They were literal remnants of a life where she had gone to an expensive boarding school, and to Oxford, and where my father had once worn a tie to work. They had been carried in trunks and marked with bookplates, *Ex Libris* printed before her maiden name. They had come across the sea. A parcel arrived one day from my Scottish grandmother, who had hardly spoken to my mother since she'd left Oxford. From layers of brown paper and string burst a red Brio train set, tiny china cups, shortbread in a tin and a set of Folio

Edition Jane Austen novels. The books were signs of a richly textured life somewhere else. Turning the thick yellow pages, the embossed leather covers, seemed more likely to get me back there than any version of romance I had access to.

Those modernist novels I liked most are often read as elitist, the selves they celebrate marked by superiority as well as alienation. The fantasies of cultural distinction that reading brought me were as powerful in their own way as those of romance. Frankie and Emma Bovary don't get out of their small towns by sleeping with men, but Frankie does get somewhere by reading: her point of view is evidence enough of a life to come. That my parents knew what books signified, even as they were busy dismantling so many other social conventions, seems possible to me as I write this now. Most readers toy with their own brands of escape. We might advocate equality or empathy but our commitment to the chances of a good reader becoming the hero of her own story is great. I do not want to risk making it sound as if books could have bootstrapped me magically out of those teenage years without the other forces that put them gently in my path.

But if reading gave me – like so many who tell of ambition's wheels greased by language – a sense of distinction, it didn't immediately point me towards middle-class life. In my later teenage years I went back to England and lived with my paternal grandmother in London, a woman very different from the one who had sent the brown-paper parcel. I hitchhiked around Europe and worked in supermarkets to pay for bread and cheese and beer. I had relationships full of drunkenness and low on any kind of romance. I went backpacking in India with a man much older than me, who knew about computers and biology. I lived with a rock guitarist who played gigs all night and slept into the afternoon. I graduated half-heartedly from a small university and regretted after-wards not having studied harder or gone somewhere better. Moved by regret, I worked overtime in a fish-and-chip shop and used the money to pay for a Masters in literary and cul-tural theory at the University of Sussex. There, intrigued by the courses I was taking, I became happy for the first time. That happiness came from meeting my whip-smart house-mate, Imogen. It also came from being good at reading and writing and talking in a setting where those things counted, and from Brighton in the early 1990s feeling like the centre of the world.

Imogen and I lived in the ground-floor flat of a house at the top of a hill above the train station. The flat was light and high-ceilinged, with three rooms that buzzed with the ringing of the phone and with visitors and music. I wrote essays on my first laptop, a square Texas Instruments machine, at a desk too big for my tiny bedroom. My window looked south, onto a seagull-filled sky and down to the station where the trains came in. From that desk I could see friends coming up the slope of the road, visitors from campus and from London and Gatwick. The person I watched out for most intensely was Hans. He was German and lived in the bigger flat upstairs with a group of anthropology students. At uni-versity talks he stood up to ask eloquent, accented questions. His hair flopped over one eye and his tweed jacket hung a little loose at his sides. He had a Danish girlfriend, an elegant person who came up that road from the station carrying hat boxes and suitcases. They were a couple from the old world, tall and blond, with things to say in public about Frankfurt School theory.

I said to Imogen: *If I ever fall in love, it will be with Hans.* It was an abstraction, a fleeting moment of insight without a plan. While many things drew me towards him, and every-thing around him, other things divided us. *He is so German*, said Imogen. *I will learn German*, I said. *He has a Danish girlfriend who looks like a movie star.* Imogen understood the dynamics of the world much better than I. Her hair was black and short, her mascara heavy, her shoe collection large. While I could imagine the past only in relation to fiction, Imogen had grown up in a family of intellectuals who wrote and appeared in books. She knew actual things: political spaces, and older men who left their wives at home to take her out for expensive drinks. Sometimes I met those men coming out of her bedroom in the mornings. Afterwards she'd lie in the bathtub, cocooned in clouds of scented foam, and tell me what it had been like.

In my courses at Sussex I read about Third World women's oppression and nineteenth-century labour move-ments. I read Friedrich Engels and Antonio Gramsci, and Richard Hoggart and Raymond Williams and Simone de Beauvoir. I thought about women fighting patriarchy, and women being free to do whatever they wanted. I swooned over Carolyn Steedman's *Landscape for a Good Woman*, in which she pinpoints with absolute clarity the fact that not all working-class women are invested in the common good, or their children. I wondered how this applied to my own mother, who had grown up with all the privileges of class and education, but renounced them to become someone making mud-bricks and cooking for a man on a shoestring budget. I wondered what class I belonged to, and who my enemy was, and which side of the divide reading literature at university put me on.

During that time I met and made friends with Clements, who was a decade older than me and taught adult education. I had delivered a paper at a student conference about the way nature appeared in eighteenth-century novels and he'd heard it and come to talk to me afterwards. He invited me to his house for dinner, led me in long strides up the lane from the train station to a worker's cottage near the River Ouse that smelled of wood-smoke. Coming into that kitchen, sitting down to eat good soup with him and his partner and their teenage children, I stumbled into a room that became as important to me over the years as any classroom. I discovered there the novels I had read from a new angle, as common reference points in generous, rambling conversations. Rather than being the girl alone with her thoughts, I became someone happy to talk about literature over a second bottle of wine.

It was in the midst of this happiness that Hans evolved for me into an actual person, someone to talk to at parties and sit next to at lectures. In a new state of confidence about myself, I kissed him on our common staircase when his girlfriend was away. I lay awake afterwards wondering what would come next. The night that followed, Hans sat on my desk and asked me to get ready for bed as if he wasn't there. He pulled up his legs as I rolled my futon out into the floor space under the desk and then undressed and stood naked in front of him. My hands at my sides, I offered my body to him, pulling an old white nightshirt slowly over my head. Hans got down from the desk and tucked me into the futon bed on the floor and kissed me and went away again upstairs. Now I could not sleep because lust and suspense and curiosity were so entangled that I could not tell them apart.

Falling in love doesn't always involve yielding to convention. Sometimes, or maybe always, it can feel like the opposite. At Sussex, for a course in 'Radical Romanticism', I read Goethe's *The Sorrows of Young Werther*. As I fell in love with Hans, I identified with Werther, a young aristocrat on holiday in the country, whose unguarded passion is transgressive and revolutionary. He meets Lotte, a woman in the neighbouring valley, when her fiancé is away in another province. Lotte is a beloved community figure, a caring older sister to her many orphaned siblings, a worthy object of devotion. Werther becomes obsessed with her. In letters to his friend he describes an all-consuming happiness: *I shall see her today! I exclaim in the mornings when I rise and look up to the beautiful sun with a glad heart; 'I shall see her today!' And then I have no other wishes all day long. Everything, everything is included in that one hope.* For months he strides feverishly around the countryside, overflowing with feelings about the grass and the sky and the children he meets, never tackling head-on the problem of Lotte being engaged to someone else. Everything Werther sees, he sees better for being in love; and everything he describes, he describes better for having Lotte in mind as his final audience.

In that context, love seems like the most powerful truth

in the world, trumping all morality and convention. Werther embodies the radical force that Austen had to reckon with in reabsorbing her lovers into society. Werther doesn't get to be with Lotte, who marries her good fiancé, as planned. Desperately unhappy, he puts on his blue coat and writes Lotte and his friends final notes, before shooting himself with her new husband's pistol. There's nothing that can be said in a casual spirit of condemnation about this suicide. Werther is surely right to love as he does, in a way that fills the world, in the assumption that even the compact unit of the family must cede ground to one who feels so much. It's the old-world morality that fails Werther, and youths like him – the true Romantics, the revolutionaries – so that Lotte and her good-hearted husband are somehow beside the point. It is said that flocks of young Germans imitated *Werther*, killing themselves and wearing blue coats in protest at a world too small for all their dreams.

A hundred years later Anna Karenina, another radical lover, also kills herself. When Anna begins an adulterous affair, her passion is undeniable; sex with Vronsky undoes her, makes her into something molten in her lover's hands; it also animates her and joins and directs her in ways she has not experienced with her husband. Once she is in love, she can't think, except of Vronsky; and to think of him is hardly thinking, it is simply letting her mind flow where it must. When he walks into a room, the whole landscape changes; and when she watches him fall from his horse, she loses all composure. Anna leaves her husband and her child to be with Vronsky. But the world cannot accommodate that passion, either, and the couple become marginal to society and eventually to each other. Anna's suicide is less imitable than Werther's, and easier to criticise. Twenty-first-century readers write in blogs about how selfish and misguided she is, how her husband was fine, what a bad mother she is (she also has a second child with Vronsky, once they are in exile). In Leo Tolstoy's nineteenth century, lovers may still be misfits, objects of readerly investment, but they cannot flaunt with the spirit of the Romantic revolutionaries the rules of society altogether.

With Hans, I felt much more like Werther than Anna. In our separate flats in that Brighton house we went on thinking and acting and leading quite different lives; we did not spend every day or take every trip together. He remained for me an exotic person to be discovered one portion at a time. I did not dare to ask when his Danish girlfriend would come home, or if he would come to my bed on any given night. But when I got up after spending a night with him, joy infused the bread I ate – the dawn crossing the sky as I rode to my early shift at the campus library, where my job was shelving books before the doors opened to the public. Being with Hans changed my conversations, in which I argued from new angles for the dignity of being a woman; and it buoyed up my encounters with other men, none of whom scared me now, because there was no one I wanted as much as Hans.

In our flat Imogen and I kept on living on fruit and wine, stealing roses for our kitchen table from the private park next door and breaking rules in our own ways. We read Engels, who describes the family as the basic unit of exploitation under capitalism. We read Barthes, who describes lovers as actors whose roles are determined for them by society, the forms of speech they use utterly unoriginal as prescriptions from Church or state. I would never have said, *I love you.* I was open to all ways of living that seemed new and unprecedented, and wanted to do anything that had not been done before. I did not see my own romance as one that would lead towards convention or even coupledom.

Yet it's hard resisting conventions in the end, hard living a life without planning a future. Falling in love does not have to produce the feeling of being in lockstep with society, yet I realised quickly that it was difficult to keep Imogen at the centre of my life while I was talking and sleeping with Hans, and that it would take a lot of effort not to worry about whether he and I were ever really to be together. After a year Hans broke up with his girlfriend without saying clearly that it was because of me. He said he wanted to do a PhD in America. Exotic letters came in through our common letterbox, piling up on the mat in the hall, offering him funded places that would take him away to Chicago or Princeton. I clung to life in England, resistant to the idea that love could change that. But when my mother came to visit, stopping in Brighton on her first, frugal trip back to the UK in decades, I blurted out to her over dinner that maybe I would go to America. *Be careful,* she warned: *do not throw it all away, do not be a sitting duck, do not trust so much in love.*

In the year after Hans left, I tried many things that had nothing to do with love. I slept with a woman with a tongue-ring, and I started writing a PhD thesis on the construction of emptiness in the colonial landscape. Imogen and I argued constantly about whether being a feminist and having the kinds of affairs she was having was harder than being a feminist and thinking of someone who was not there. I was not bereft without Hans. I did not need him to take me anywhere. But the thing less obvious in *The Member of the Wedding* than the critique of the couple is that Frankie is not really alone. While it's no secret in the novel that the young girl, like Emma, is wrong to count on romance as something that will sweep her away, in subtler ways the novel itself proves her right to want a dialogue so deep and true that it might cancel out the isolation she feels as a teenager in a small town. The proof of that conversation is the way McCullers opens up Frankie's mind and shares it with us. That is the actual intimacy that *The Member of the Wedding* models, giving Frankie to us through a narrator who overhears her thoughts and tells them as naturally as one lover might offer her fears or hopes to another.

It was Austen who did that kind of overhearing first, inventing a narrator blessed with the capacity to know everything, the blasts of prejudice and longing, and the secret thoughts of women shut up in houses in the countryside. Austen passes this all on to us in confidence, in the mood of shared cleverness and conspiracy, in an intimacy that becomes evidence of her readers being able to rise with her above their own provincial worlds. In this spirit, Austen often suggests that love is not everything it's made out to be. There are plenty of signs it might be limited or go wrong. Austen gets her favourite characters to the altar with dignity and verve intact, without saying much about how those well-matched couples are meant to go on sharing their thoughts or their lives. She shows us scenes of courtship while reserving judgement about the reality of waking every day of one's life with an ageing Darcy. She does nothing to guarantee that Elizabeth and Darcy will not become like her older married couples, bickering and bored in the background of a new generation's romance. The only faith she really insists we keep is with the state of confidence that she establishes with her reader. Austen's inviting us to believe in the fact that we might one day fall in love depends less on the way Emma loves Knightley than on the way she loves us, the ones with whom she shares the story.

That character of Austen's narrator – so composed, so perfectly tuned in to her characters – is no simple model of the kind of company one would want to keep. Austen's voice has been described by the critic D. A. Miller as the embodiment of style. In this context it is also a model of exclusion from the institutions of marriage that she represents, a paean to the kinds of self-sufficiency and self-consciousness gay men might aspire to. But that stylish narrator is so intimate with her characters. It is because of her that their thoughts seem so neatly plucked and given to us. Elizabeth, wandering around Pemberley before meeting Darcy on his home turf, *was overpowered by shame and vexation. Her coming there was the most unfortunate, the most ill-judged thing in the world!* In technical terms, the second of these sentences shifts into free, indirect narration. The narrator begins to 'do' Elizabeth's voice without losing her own. In fact Elizabeth's being at Pemberley, in Darcy's way, is not bad at all. That is merely a thought Elizabeth has, delivered up to us with the wit of a friend who knows everything she thinks.

In those first years with Hans and Imogen, I stayed

uncertain about the conventions and loyalties of love, but I grew committed to that idea of full-throttle communication. More than social distinction or class privilege, it was this that I had learned in all those years of having narrators whispering in my ear, trusting that I was laughing about the wedding scenes, trusting that minds could be known to each other. My desperate desire to be in that kind of conversation came from feeling Goethe's narrator saying, *let us call this character Edvard*, while pouring me a drink and setting up a fictional world for my benefit on the table between us. It came from feeling that my relationship with Jane Eyre would be happier than any she would ever have with Rochester. It came from knowing that when Austen wrote those famous opening lines of *Pride and Prejudice* – *It is a truth universally acknowledged, that a single man in possession of a good fortune, must be in want of a wife* – she was taking on someone else's voice, and trusting I would know that.

So much of the reading I did as a teenager involved gathering evidence that social conformity wasn't worth it. But that gathering established my intimacy with a team of first-person narrators who saved me from being alone: Jane Eyre, Holden Caulfield, Jean Louise Finch, Plath's Esther Greenwood, Daphne, the narrator of Janet Frame's first novel *Owls Do Cry*. I believed so fully in that possibility of radical intimacy that I followed it far, away from Imogen, from England, from my mother's advice, off into the world. If pressed, I would say that I still believe in it, would still go anywhere for the experience of having a voice talking to me the way Austen's narrator talks to her reader.

I got on that plane to Newark having spent all winter

writing to Shannon of everything around me: the grass, the bread, my children, my marriage, the reasons I feared the conversation we were having. I emptied my mind into hers without realising how much there was still to say. Novels may not have helped me know what I was going to do next, or what it meant to fall in love with someone so deeply at this late juncture of my life, but they had taught me to celebrate the romance of words that I was having now, again, with someone who'd read even more of them than I had.

CHAPTER THREE

MARRIAGE AND ITS LIMITS

Many people see marriage linking us to the past. Something that makes sense because people have been doing it for so long. But companionate marriage wasn't always conventional. That idea that a man and wife should share experiences, move in similar circles, go on a honeymoon alone and live together more or less as equals remained innovative late into the eighteenth century. Visitors from the continent commented on the oddity of British wives being seen so much out and about with their husbands. Conduct manuals carefully elucidated the new principles of conjugal life and conversation as new things to be grasped and understood. Peeking out from behind the scenes of Austen's romances are other ways of living obscured by fiction's focus on conjugality: as an adulterer, a polygamist, under the protection of a father, in intimate connection with a sister, as an unhappy spouse. Austen's plots may be intricately rigged towards the pairing up of characters in love, but her worlds are full of secondary characters excluded from or ill served by marriage.

Even as companionate marriage has been championed by novelists, religious writers and moralists, it's had a steadfast string of critics. There were people who stuck to other ways of life: the servants and labourers who simply couldn't afford to marry; plenty of regular aristocrats who used it to secure an income rather than as a matter of the heart; and spouses who found their romance and their pleasure outside the conjugal bed. Others thought that marriage, however freely chosen, could never be revolutionary enough. Mary Wollstonecraft and William Godwin were some of the institution's most scandalous ideological detractors and both wrote openly in the 1790s of marriage as an institution that embodied the problems of monarchy and dictatorship on a personal scale. Godwin decried it as *the worst of all laws* – one that committed citizens to continuity when they should be embracing change. Contracting promises you couldn't keep was counter-productive, in his mind, to making citizens for a new world. If men were forced to become liars and hypocrites in the private domain, what kind of freedom could they hope to gain? The whole capacity for radical thought was infected, in Godwin's terms, by the error involved in trying to make the future answerable to the past.

Wollstonecraft argued with equal vehemence that marriage supported lives of legalised prostitution for women, depriving them of the chance to contribute actively to society. In her fiction, she represented brutal marriages from which there was no escape, and she pursued in practice her own versions of free love. At one point she suggested to Imlay, her American lover and the father of her daughter, Fanny, that they live together with the actress he'd fallen in love with. Imlay declined, sending Mary instead to investigate business dealings in Scandinavia that had gone wrong.

Her *Letters Written in Sweden, Norway and Denmark* is a book about that journey and, when Godwin read it, he declared it a narrative bound to make the reader fall in love with its author. When Wollstonecraft returned to London, the two became lovers while keeping separate houses in the same London street. At three or four, Fanny was able to run between them with notes written by her mother about nights of pleasure still strong in her veins. *Don't feed her too many sweets* when she arrives with this letter at your house, her mother reminded Godwin. The two didn't marry until Wollstonecraft's second pregnancy was well under way, by which time giving in to convention only made the scandal of their relationship worse.

Perhaps Godwin and Wollstonecraft felt disorientated by being married in the way that Hans and I did when we ended up living together in 1997. We'd held out for so long against common plans and fixed promises that it was strange to find ourselves there among people who took tradition and coupledom so seriously. During the year that I stayed with Imogen in Brighton, Hans wrote to me from America of his new life of bagels, friends with therapy appointments, classes on post-structuralism. Princeton was a town of suburban streets lined with trees that moulted bright autumn leaves, and a library that stayed open all night. He lived on its outskirts in a field of housing rented to international graduate students. Built quickly in the 1940s for students coming to study under the GI Bill, the Butler barracks criss-crossed in what was meant to be a temporary formation a field once used for polo matches. Hans wrote to me on airmail paper of wild nights in the graduate student bar, and of the house being small and functional, heated with a breathy fan that pumped warm air into it a few times an hour.

I convinced myself that moving there to join him was in my own interests; that the education I'd get by starting graduate school again, with classes and committees, would make up for all the school I'd missed as a teenager. Getting my fellowship to Rutgers, the university down the road from Hans, and moving across the Atlantic to be with him didn't feel like the absolute concession to love that my mother feared. I knew where my priorities lay. In my application statement I said every wrong thing about wanting to change the world – maybe to live in India or work part-time growing vegetables while reading Marx and Gramsci in the afternoons – and spelt Nietzsche without a Z. I spent the summer before I arrived having a dark and passionate affair with a Marxist writer I'd met in Berlin, who couldn't imagine why any life on the other side of the Atlantic, where there was no state to speak of, would be worth migrating for.

Hans and I left England well versed in radical texts about class inequality. But these weren't the main lines of study at the American universities we joined. We began our life together in the US in the middle of a decade of vibrant queer politics, after a decade of the AIDS crisis in New York. My first courses at Rutgers involved reading Queer Theory with charismatic teachers, drinking with fellow students who were passionate about their identities and sexuality in ways I'd never encountered before. With those people I read Eve Kosofsky Sedgwick and Michael Warner and the novelists of loneliness that I would later learn Shannon liked: Radclyffe Hall, Sarah Orne Jewett, Willa Cather. In Princeton, where

Hans studied anthropology, Judith Butler gave high-profile lectures on alternative modes of kinship.

The question of how my own love life fitted into all that I was reading was complicated. On the one hand, Hans and I were rapidly becoming a straight couple in our late twenties, perpetrators of the kind of domestic arrangement that the theory we were reading railed against. On the other, we stayed less interested in the imperatives of conjugal life than many of the people we met. We didn't plan to have houses or jobs or children in the ways that some of our queer friends did. I remember listening quizzically to a fellow student, a gay man, telling me about his desire to adopt, asking my advice about the timing of parenthood. Many of the people I met were fighting for gay marriage, which wouldn't be legalised for more than a decade in the United States. As a straight woman, I had nothing good to say about marriage as an institution. I viewed it critically as a financial arrangement that was exploitative of domestic labour, unfair in its distribution of property and weak in its collective vision of life. I liked Jeanette Winterson's description in *Written on the Body* of marriage as a plate-glass window just begging for a brick.

To one of her early emails, Shannon attached proofs of an article in which she observed that something was lost in that first decade of the twenty-first century for queers and feminists alike: *Getting married and having kids pose some significant challenges to those who forged a sense of self not only outside the family but also against it.* Reading that reminded me of those years in New Jersey when Hans and I were united in our opposition to marriage. It was only when Marie was born in 2002 that we rethought our position. We had gone back to Germany for her birth, which came many weeks too early, and stayed on afterwards in the Danish farmhouse that Hans and his best friend owned. We spent the last months of that summer on the island, without running water or phones, washing baby clothes of the smallest size by hand and hanging them out to dry in the sun. As happy as Marie's company made us, and as creatively as we shared her care, having her bound us together in new ways. How were we ever going to read and write again with so much extra work to do? How could we live apart now? We were due back to the US to finish our theses, but Hans's visa and funding had already run out and my visa wouldn't get him back into the country. *You'd best just get married*, said the university immigration officer looking at our case, incredulous that we hadn't thought of it already.

We announced the wedding over breakfast at the farmhouse to friends visiting from Germany – a human-rights activist who had once been Hans's girlfriend, and Hans's brother, who was visiting from an anarchist collective in Hamburg. At lunchtime a councillor drove up the dirt road, parked her car and performed a no-nonsense ceremony in which she underscored the fact that relationships were hard work. Our friends bought us a kite from the local shop, and cooked lunch with vegetables from the stall down the road. The wind made the light-green leaves stand up, and a hedgehog crossed the edge of the field. The white shirt I'd put on got smeared with breast milk. The sky was completely clear of cloud, and we went for a walk that afternoon with Marie tied in a cloth to Hans's belly, the island lying like a great creature floating in the sea.

In that moment, even as we began parenting Marie together, we had no fixed sense of the domestic life we wanted. Back in the US, I spoke out during graduate-school meetings in favour of the adjunct and community-college teaching positions that were presented only as poor standby options for professorial careers. I felt passionate about having time to care for others, and suspicious about professional success. I coveted the life of Clements and his partner back in Sussex, cooking meals made from vegetables grown on their allotment, translating radical philosophy between languages. Clements and I often talked about Thomas Hardy, a writer we both admired, especially his *Jude the Obscure*, a novel about a working-class man who wants to study at the elite university. *We forget those years when Jude is lucky in the life he has*, Clements observed, *as a craftsman and parent, a man literate in so many things that matter more than Latin texts*. Jude is remembered mostly for the bitter failures of his life, and the novel for its tragic denouement.

Clements is right: for the years covered most lightly in that novel, Jude lives happily together with his partner, Sue. He works as an itinerant stonemason, and Sue helps him sometimes in painting the letters he carves in stone. They take care of the son from Jude's first marriage and have two children of their own. Even when Jude becomes sick, he works from home, baking cakes in the shapes of the spires and cathedrals from the university town he loves, which Sue sells successfully at local fairs. Jude fails as a scholar of Latin, but he does so in the era of education becoming more democratic. Local reading clubs and evening classes were on the rise in late nineteenth-century Britain and he has access to these in the towns, where he and Sue stop to work. Having each been catastrophically married before, Jude and Sue themselves do not marry. But even here, in his most bitter novel, Hardy recognises this simple fact that life led, day after day, with someone you love can be well irrigated with happiness.

Fiction rarely does justice to the quality of days and weeks and years spent together, to the rhythms that comfort, the agreed-upon ways of folding laundry, roasting potatoes, running a bath. No matter where we lived, and how unconventional we felt as partners, Hans always left a light on over our front steps for me when it got late, a kind of beacon. The light was there at the end of a night out or a trip to another city. It did not ask anything of me – not explanation, and only rarely apology. Even after meeting Shannon I kept walking along the paved street that led to our Copenhagen flat with a sense of relief and hope. That home was where sleep came to me most deeply, my breaths mingled with others, all those strands of familiarity and attachment thickening the air.

That mundane kind of happiness is on show in a rare way in James Salter's *Light Years*. Published in 1975, it follows the life of Viri and Nedra, a married couple living with their two daughters in a converted barn on the Hudson in the 1950s and 60s. It can feel embarrassing to invoke characters so ridiculously beautiful, so financially well cushioned, as these mid-century Americans, with their casual relationships to tailored shirts and Long Island summers. It's the detail that Salter makes the subject of *Light Years* – the dinner-party menus, the father and child stopping to watch the tops of carrots disappear into the mouth of the pet rabbit, the collectively chosen sofa cushions, the exhaustion after a children's party and its puppet show, the laying of the fire, the relaxing of bodies that know each other when the fire has gone out and the friends have left.

All this cataloguing would simply be smug if Salter didn't also get the panning-out right, the spiral of Christmases and summers, flinging the kids towards adulthood. My life with Hans built up so many ways of over-layering the weeks and the years. On that Danish island where we got married, we rode down a stretch of bike path by the sea every summer for decades, with different combinations of wheels and baby seats and tag-alongs, succeeded by kids on their own bikes beside us and then out ahead. The pleasure of the swooping coastline piled up as we came back and back to it, making following it an act of remembering and anticipating. Our life seemed riveted there, at that intersection of space and time. *Let's stop at that place*, one of us would say, and we would eat sandwiches and remember what they had tasted like the year before. In *Light Years*, Nedra and Viri go to Long Island every year. Viri watches his daughters swimming in the waves, sees himself reflected with one of them in a shop window as if already looking from the future. Domestic time capsules itself into meaningful building blocks.

One problem with these descriptions of family life, and one reason to avoid them, is the almost inevitably cruel performance in which they catch us up. Salter writes of Viri and Nedra's marriage as two things: *it was a life, more or less – at least it was a preparation for one – and it was an illustration of a life for their children. They had never expressed this to one another, but they were agreed upon it, and these two versions were entwined somehow so that one being hidden, the other was revealed.* Light Years participates in this account of couple-dom by making the intimate details of family life those most easily offered up for display. Even before social media made an art of such self-presentation, I sometimes took pleasure in broadcasting images of my family summers, writing to my mother or my friends to make sure they saw me as someone who had a place in the frame of what might just pass as a stock photo or a school-reunion notice. Look: here I am, on holiday with my husband, our children, eating cherries from the tree, the sea in the background. No sign of the fights, the confusion over where we should live or how much work we should each be doing.

Shannon had taken, and starred in and produced, plenty of family pictures of her own by the time I met her. Yet in her first flurry of letters to me that winter she described the feeling that a married life like mine was designed to exclude someone like her. Historically, I understood what she was saying about family life having been fortressed through representation against spinsters, gays, fallen women, hucksters, criminals and refugees – all the people it banished to the outside. I understood the rage of that swashbuckling, gender-queer, plate-glass-smashing narrator of Winterson's *Written on the Body*, who spits on the married couple: *The self-exhibition, the self-satisfaction, swarminess, tightness, tight-arsedness.* But when it came to our specifics, I felt she was wrong. It was true that Hans and I enjoyed the kinds of protection that heterosexuality and whiteness and education bring. But we were also broad-minded children of the 1970s, unsentimental about the family and open to doing things differently. Did marriage always have to shut someone out?

The idea of the nuclear family as a charmed scene, a place of desire and happy endings, was launched early in the history of the novel, even before the marriage plot became its mainstay. In the decades before Austen and Wollstonecraft wrote, the most faddish fiction coerced its readers into a state of sentimental response: unfortunate orphans, beguiling beggars, kitchen hearths, loving mothers with infants, and children with puppies could all do the trick. This trade in feeling was offset by more rational arguments that Wollstonecraft and Godwin and their revolutionary peers made. But sentiment was still instrumental in promoting causes they shared. These included the abolition of slavery, the advance of human and animal rights and the promotion of the working family. A line of continuity runs from novels like *The Vicar of Wakefield*, a popular fiction of 1766, through Dickens and a host of nineteenth-century writers who celebrate the nuclear family, all the way to *Light Years* in its more sentimental moments. I was never told I should grow up and get married, but I spent years reading and rereading *Little House on the Prairie*, noting the glory of being tucked up safely in bed while Ma sews and Pa strums on the guitar. As Shannon would point out, there's no doubt that such scenes, legitimately desirable as they can seem, have always felt safe partly because they provide protection from the wrong kind of stranger. There's nothing like the scene of a warm and well-fed family to make the lines between inside and outside painfully obvious. The light burning on the windowsill, or above the stairs, has never burned for everyone. The nuclear family is repellent in this sense of the very kinds of libido and longing that it takes, in moderate quantities, to keep it going.

I first read James Baldwin's *Another Country*, which is about a group of friends in New York, in a mood of optimism about how much the family could include. We were in Princeton and I was pregnant with Marie. Love runs in all directions in that 1960s novel – between musicians and writers, male friends, bodies of different identities and colours, across the Atlantic from Europe to the US, right through the middle of the nuclear family. The one married couple in the novel, Richard and Cass, are not its most appealing protagonists, but they are the spot where many lines of desire meet: the desire to become a writer, the desire for a home, the desire for Cass, often seen preparing drinks while Richard writes and entertains, as a published author. While it may not be good, their marriage is a conduit of wider circuits of lust and sociability, attributes that I imagined should flow through houses and the families they contained.

Shannon and her friends read that novel quite differently from me in the 1990s. For a start, they were reading it together, in a spirit more resonant of the novel's real emphasis on friendship. It is true, as I wanted to imagine, that Richard and Cass are the locus for the less conventional encounters that spread out into the world of Baldwin's novel. Cass is a bright spot, desired and desiring, receptive and awake, despite her status as mother and wife. But the real stress in *Another Country* is on the connections spread across the novel through Rufus, who is a friend to most of its characters. To the extent that marriage is a focal point for Baldwin, it is a bond among others, more limited in the end than the plural bonds between friends. In my second reading of the novel I followed Rufus's friend, Vivaldo, more closely. He lives together with Ida, Rufus's beautiful sister, in a small East Village apartment. Vivaldo is writing a novel that promises vaguely to become this one that we are reading. Ida is trying to make it as a singer, a woman whose blackness makes her doubly vulnerable to the predatory white men running the music industry.

Still, the problem of representing the family home – any family, any home – without excluding someone is not entirely resolved, even in *Another Country*. Vivaldo and Ida are a more radical couple than Richard and Cass. But they are still a couple, domestically a unit from which other people can feel shut out. Their home is different from the one in *Little House on the Prairie*, but it's not open to everyone. On hot summer nights there's the dilemma of whether to open the front door to their apartment. If they don't, it is stifling inside, and they drive each other mad with their competing notes of conflict and support. Yet when they do open the door to the landing, the whole city seems to look in at them with desire and curiosity. People listen to Ida sing, or stop to watch her lying on the sofa in her blue playsuit. One night Vivaldo catches a lonely boy on the landing with his hands deep inside his trousers and chases him away in disgust. Even in a novel as generous as this in its affordances, only some people get to be on the inside. To close the door on any kind of arrangement is stifling, but to expose it to view is to risk creating yet another world of aroused and ostracised onlookers.

I felt this paradox at work when reading *The Argonauts*, Maggie Nelson's first-person account of queer love and marriage and parenting. I galloped through that book soon after it came out in 2015. Nelson and her trans partner Harry are parents to a baby and to Harry's son from an earlier relationship. They put up a swing and fold small socks, sit happily on the red sofa. Nelson is not exactly at home with all this domesticity: she marbles it well with details of their sex and edgier, more public ways of life. But *The Argonauts* is, at its simplest, the story of a happy couple at home with their kids. A bestseller among those readers I know, it is as effective in making the queer family enviable from the outside as any novel has been in making the hearth feel like the place to be. When Shannon pointed out to me how happy my photos looked, I remembered the way I had felt as a straight person reading Nelson describe the many desires, the baby and books she has lined up under one roof. Being queer and married and so wanted by Harry, she seemed to have it all. Nelson knows that their happiness becomes a problem once it's put on display, writes of the way her friends feel about the tacky family photos on show in her house, but she doesn't have a fix for the problem.

Hans and I probably seemed from the outside at our most married when we lived in our tin-clad house in Ann Arbor. Tall and ugly from the kerb, it let light into its rooms generously right through the day. For a few years when we lived there we had a garden, friends, kids, our own stretch of the pavement to be cleared of leaves and snow. Hans built a fireplace. We planted vegetables and flowers in beds raised up off the lawn, and sat and watched fireflies in the garden at night. Marie acted in plays at the YMCA and went to summer sailing camp at a lake. Rohan took his first teetering steps on the grass, which we mowed on weekends with an oversized machine. The back bedroom of that house had a deck, where I liked to sit reading and watching the neighbours. From there, we might have kept going – teaching, harvesting, getting the kids into colleges, going back to Europe in the summer.

During those years I puzzled over the dearth of novels about happy couples. I was planning to write a book of literary criticism that would address head-on that question of why fictional plots so rarely represent married life. When people talk about marriage as fiction's standard happy ending, they often forget how few novels actually describe life after the wedding. Given their professional commitment to getting characters paired up, novelists, I thought, were strikingly uninterested in keeping them together. *Name one novel for me*, I dared my friends, *where a couple are just happy together – where they simply get to live, and get old and stay happy, without adultery or disaster striking.* My colleagues who studied the eighteenth-century novel came up with the example of Henry's Fielding's *Amelia*, a slightly sentimental novel written as tribute to his much-loved second wife. Everyone else seemed stuck for ideas. Perhaps the couple in *Light Years*, before they get divorced? Perhaps Austen?

But Austen, I pointed out, *always stops in her tracks when it comes to marriage.* In the last pages of *Northanger Abbey*, her narrator jokes about the evidence of a plot coming to its close. Anxiety about the outcome, the narrator quips, *can hardly extend, I fear, to the bosom of my readers, who will see from the tell-tale compression of the pages before them, that we are all hastening together to perfect felicity.* She's pointing to the kind of happy ending she was helping to normalise, making a joke about the romance, as well as about the way a book puts the married couple physically in our hands. The future in a novel is always already there, waiting for us to turn the pages. Except that there are never enough pages to keep a marriage going. Austen herself never actually treats that predictability of plot as anything except a reason to set down her pen: here's a romance and a wedding, but if you want a happy marriage, she says with an eyebrow cocked, you'll have to imagine it.

In one early-morning session of work in my university office, a cooling pint of latte on my desk, I realised that it's not so much that novelists avoid writing about marriage, as that the topic forces them to wrestle with the predictability of their medium: the book, the genre of the novel, the expectations of plot and the happy ending. In real life there's no way to guarantee that love will last. There's a sleight of hand involved in real people promising to love anyone for ever, an unexpected side to reality that contracts can't withstand. Hardy points this out in *Jude the Obscure*, which delivers up one of the most scathing accounts of a wedding ever written. How pointless it is for Jude and Arabella to swear *that at every other time of their lives till death took them, they would assuredly believe, feel, and desire precisely as they had believed, felt, and desired during the preceding weeks.* How much uncertainty and statistical improbability those making and witnessing the marriage vows elide. *What was as remarkable as the undertaking itself,* points out Hardy's narrator scathingly, *was the fact that nobody seemed at all surprised at what they swore.*

Despite his celebrated portrait of Werther's romantic feeling, Goethe was similarly alert to the hypocrisy in promising that love would last. He lived with the working-class Christiane Vulpius, mother to his many children, for seventeen years before they married in 1806. When she died, he had engraved on her tombstone: *the whole gain of my life is to weep over her loss.* But he saw it as a downfall to take that longevity of love, or the social normality of the couple, for granted. Perhaps he remained true to Werther, the character of his youth, who had found the absoluteness of Lotte's marriage so hard to take. In later letters and essays, Goethe represented marriage as the work of squaring a messy reality with an impossible ideal. *It is good that such examples exist,* he conceded, *because in postulating the impossible one strives for the most possible.* The married couple, though unlikely to succeed, are heroic nonetheless in their efforts.

Novelists, though, face a problem different from those promising in real life to stay together. In a book, it's easy to make fictional love run smooth. Novel worlds are rigged towards the kind of predictability that couples at the altar can only dream of. Getting married in real life is only ever a hypothesis. But a novelist really *can* make anything happen. If a novel begins with the announcement that a happy couple will stay together, then they will. Fielding experiments with this when he opens *Amelia* as a history that *concerns the various accidents which befel a very worthy couple after their uniting in the state of matrimony.* The novel throws all kinds of challenges in Booth and Amelia's way – poverty, infidelity, extramarital desire, imprisonment – but it stubbornly preserves the couple as its subject. We know that Booth and Amelia will stay together, because Fielding has promised it. It's reassuring, but hardly a reason to keep reading.

More familiar is a page-turning scenario like the one faced by Roy and Celeste, lead characters in Tayari Jones's 2018 *An American Marriage*. Like Amelia and Booth 250 years earlier, Roy and Celeste really do like each other. And, like the earlier couple, they are both attractive and flirtatious and full of life. But Roy ends up in prison, convicted because he's black rather than because he's guilty of the rape he is accused of. The couple write to each other for years before Celeste moves on. The tragedy is tragically credible. In sociological terms, racism, injustice and poverty too often undermine romantic promises that get made. But they are not the main forces driving fictional couples apart. In novels, as Fielding shows, married people can just stay married. Hardy could have honoured the naïve belief of Jude and Arabella's wedding guests by having them stick it out. Jones is not compelled by statistics to part the couple she has invented. In novels about marriage, divorce strikes less because of human inconsistency or injustice than because tragic events must offset what would otherwise be uniquely foreseeable about a fictional future.

So Jones sends Roy to prison, just as Hardy, a century earlier, has Jude's marriage to Arabella end before their first year is out. Arabella leaves for Australia, and Jude for Christminster, the university city that he longs to be part of. There he finds Sue engaged to Phillotson, his old schoolmaster.

Sue's marriage fails even more dramatically than Jude's to Arabella, with Phillotson conceding after many unhappy months of platonic cohabitation that Sue should go and be with Jude. She and Jude end up on the road together with his blessing. Now they might just stay together. Jude and Sue see themselves as *queer sorts*, but even such a couple of outsiders can stay true to each other. Hardy again has it in his power to make new promises stick.

And this is fiction: Hardy could have summoned up the future, allowed Jude and Sue to live unmarried, nourishing each other intellectually and sexually without having to promise that, or make it an advertisement for others to do the same. It was not long in historical terms before de Beauvoir and Sartre lived in this spirit; before Baldwin went to Paris and fell in love with young men; before the English socialist and early gay activist Edward Carpenter took George Merrill to live with him in Derbyshire, getting buried at his side in a Surrey cemetery in 1929. It is because they are characters in a novel that Jude and Sue attract disaster of a special kind. Arriving back in Christminster one rainy afternoon, the family looks for lodgings. Sue, heavily pregnant with their third child, is admitted to a boarding house along with the children, and Jude goes off to spend the night in a cheap tavern. Overcome with a characteristic fit of honesty, Sue confesses to her landlady that she and Jude are unmarried, that they remain terrified that *the conditions of the contract should kill their love*. The landlady responds to this by saying that they must leave the house the next day.

In the midst of this crisis, Jude and Sue care well for each other. Jude lies sleepless in his tavern worrying about Sue and the unborn child. And Sue lies awake wondering how to break the news of their eviction to Jude, who is still recovering from his own illness. Early the next morning she goes to his tavern for breakfast and they talk, taking some eggs with them when they leave. Back in Sue's rooms, Jude cooks the eggs on a small stove, and Sue goes into the inner chamber to wake the children. There's something about those details that recalls all the years Hans and I spent packing, moving on, arriving in new places, finding ways to feed and shelter everyone, apart and together. The collaboration of adults against the background of children eating and growing, sleeping and waking, describes what it can be like. I feel that swoop of the bikes under us as we move along the coastal path. But the pages are ticking away as the eggs are boiling, and Jude is timing them, and so the children are already dead. In real life, children normally wake up and complain about not liking their breakfast, and their parents chide gently, knowing that at least there is something to eat. Even when children die, couples sometimes work it out together, as Jude implores Sue to stay and do. Hans always hated Hardy. We had, over the years, a series of conversations in which he made his aversion to such tragic endings clear.

Books and their genres tend formally and conventionally towards the view from above. Readers of novels know much more about what's going on than we ever do in real life, about what is likely to happen next, about where things will end. But readers pay for this point of view by being primed for accident and disaster, for plot. Constitutionally, as readers, it's that uncertainty that we expect, and the tragedy that we remember. *Anna Karenina* could have been about Kitty and Levin, the couple who get to live happily at the end of that novel. Yet it's Anna and Vronsky whose storyline everyone can recount. Roy and Celeste's story is not remembered for their time of bantering intimacy, but because they fall victim to a hideously unjust system. No underwriter would approve an insurance policy taken out on the well-being of married, fictional protagonists.

In this sense, meeting Shannon felt from the outset more like part of a novel than the happiest parts of my life with Hans. A friend, an accomplished writer of stories of modern life, observed when I blurted out that I had met someone: *You sound so happy. But I think*, she said, stirring her cup, *maybe you are now an ice-skater, swooping elegantly across an almost-certainly-frozen lake with a glass of champagne in your hand.* Another colleague, a man I knew less well, heard rumours and said, *You never cease to surprise me, Tina.* He had the hair of a rogue and had just left his wife for a younger woman. But it was my plot twist he wanted to talk about. *You are always doing what no one expects*, he said. *What are you going to do now?* asked Hans, less happily, as we discussed how it might all work. *Are you just going to leave – to disappear? If she is your soulmate, will you even come back from New York?* I had become a character likely to slip, change course, experience great unhappiness. In putting my marriage in question, I became for the first time in years a person within a plot.

Yet this truth is difficult to square with that other axiom, which is that novels advocate married life, prime us to want its satisfactions and securities. For twenty-five years Hans and I lived within those norms of fiction. Not only in our infidelities and our lives in different cities, but in our pleasures, our rituals, our long years of childcare, our ordinariness. These are the qualities of experience that stick most couples together. The pleasure of feeding carrot tops to the rabbit. Of planning and making dinner. Of swimming in the river with the current on your side. When novels try and record that, it often comes across as background. It's a struggle to remember that *Anna Karenina* ends with Kitty telling Levin to go and check on the bedding in the guest room, rather than with Anna dead on the railway tracks. But these are the qualities of life that novels have often been thought to promote, at least in their more conservative emphasis on the couple and the family and that way of life within the home.

Beethoven was not married, nor was Flaubert, observes Hardwick in *Sleepless Nights*. Writing from beyond her own marriage, she advocates for the divorcees, the bachelors, the female friends, the queer artists of the city. *Voltaire lived thirty years longer than his mistress and Dr Johnson thirty after Elizabeth. Both lived out life in a populated singleness.* Hardwick, more diplomatic than Lowell about their life together, does not say much about what she has left behind. At only one point in *Sleepless Nights* does she give us this: *I was then a 'we'.* There were evenings in which *nothing subtle or interesting* was said. *Husband-wife: not a new move to be discovered in that strong classical tradition. Arguments are like the grinding of rusty blades, the old motor and its troublesome knockings. The dog growls. He too knows his lines.* Fair enough. Lowell trusted her to deal with the car insurance, the property taxes, their daughter's education, the sorting out of the housemaid, plane tickets, medical treatment. He wrote his poems in his own studio a block down the road and, when he left New York for pastoral England, she had to find a tenant for that property. For Hardwick, along with the pain of divorce came reprieve, space to breathe, time to write.

Sometimes the very existence of the novel seems to depend on marriage ending, its scenes of domestic concord being left behind, or seen from above. This is especially true, I think, of fiction written by women, as if their imbrication in marriage were always a great threat to them having anything to say. Reading Doris Lessing and other twentieth-century women of whom it is said that they *left their husbands to write*, I have wondered if that is something people might ever say about me. It is ironic yet true that it is hard for a story to emerge, to exist at all, among domestic settings and routines that fiction has helped to celebrate. Many friends have envied me my life of commuting, two nights alone every week away from my kids, with access to the Swedish house in the forest.

From the beginning, Austen intuited that unmarried life might be better for those who hope to spend their days reading and writing by the window, observing others, skipping dinner. Intimacy with narrators may be a thing we want, a model for falling in love, but almost as soon as writers begin to appear as characters in fiction, their well-being seems threatened by the domestic crowd. In one eighteenth-century text the poet paces the cobblestones, taking down notes to use later when the children are asleep and there is peace to write at home. Pamela, fictional author of her own story, is only able to write all those letters because she's locked away: once she's married and absorbed with daily life, her story disintegrates. Godfrey St Peter, hero of Willa Cather's *The Professor's House*, keeps his old study after his family's new house is built in order to have a place in which to write and dream of a young man he used to know. In middle age St Peter finds himself landlocked, immobilised by marriage, unable to capture what it was that once gave him joy in writing. Anna, of Doris Lessing's *The Golden Notebook*, is a single mother struggling to write a book in a setting where her life is fractured between different notebooks and roles that she must play.

George Gissing's *New Grub Street*, written late in the nineteenth century, was one of the first things Clements urged me to read. It describes a group of writers struggling to make a living in London. Like all of Gissing's novels, it involves a slightly bitter doubling-down on the unfairness of class, on the worker's exclusion from the creation of art. Set just a few years earlier than *Jude the Obscure*, the book casts most of Gissing's characters as aspiring writers who work in fear of poverty, minimally employed as reviewers and novelists and newspaper journalists. Women with inky hands spend their lives as copyists and amanuenses for their fathers and spouses. The central character in the novel, Edwin Reardon, has enjoyed some early success as a novelist before marrying Amy, a respectable and ambitious helpmate. Being married takes a greater toll on his art than he could have imagined. He worries about the bills, struggles to describe to Amy what he's doing. He writes restlessly at his desk while Amy and the child break the silence that ought to be his right. In frustration and impending poverty, he sells the furniture, dismantles the family home. Amy goes off in relief to live with her mother, and Reardon reverts to a bachelor existence. He is poor and miserable, but even so, Gissing suggests, better set now for writing a good novel than he was in the conjugal home.

I knew Clements didn't feel like that about his own writing or his life in his personally and intellectually full house, but then his years of parenting small children were mostly over when I met him. Some of the stories he told me about what his life had been when the children were small suggested that he might have liked a room of his own then. The materiality of literature as something that gets read and written and made under certain conditions rather than others has been often present in our conversations. Virginia Woolf argued famously that fiction by women will not really emerge until they have their own space and time. Even characters like Clarissa Dalloway and Mrs Ramsey, materially well off and so profound in their mental landscapes, appear in this light as people who could not have written about their married lives if Woolf hadn't been there, with her own privileges of solitude, to do it for them. Perhaps it is because writing from within a marriage is so hard – even when the marriage does not involve actual cooking and childcare, even when it involves daily joy – that so few novels exist to represent the sustainability of that life.

Even *Another Country*, that novel so porous to many loves and lusts, sets limits on the sociability of the writer. The fact that Richard is writing while married to Cass is somehow to blame for the mediocrity of his first novel, and Vivaldo has a hard time writing with Ida in the room. He struggles with his typewriter while Ida travels through the range of her voice. While she sings, he fails to write; and while he writes, she paces the room, brings him beer, lights him cigarettes he doesn't want. The orchestras playing in their heads clash and compete for space and time: *on the evenings they were together in the house, he really could not work, for he could not move far enough away from her, he could not enter himself.* The novel we are reading needs to come from somewhere, and the sense that Baldwin must be alone in order to write it is as strong as the tensions of race and gender driving his couples apart.

Sitting on the deck of the Ann Arbor house, when the meetings were over and the kids asleep and Hans was working on his own book (not strumming the guitar, like Pa in *Little House on the Prairie*), I read a lot of novels in search of one that would make marriage seem sustainable and compatible with a life of writing and reading. At the time this seemed like an academic quest, tied up with a formal question that I had about why marriage and fiction were so structurally opposed. But, looking back, perhaps I also wanted to understand why daily life with Hans in that white house did not make us happier. Our ambitions had become so tied up with getting things written and professional things achieved. But our own sense of a new world, a better one, was lagging. There was hardly time left to imagine it.

One of the stories about married people I relished in that setting was Ali Smith's *The Accidental.* There Michael, a professor poet, and Eve, a writer of historical fiction, are on holiday in Norfolk with Eve's teenage kids. Neither character is particularly likeable. They lie in bed at night fighting over a pillow, making tea for each other after a bad dream, having perfectly good sex when both are turned on by a stranger, a woman, who has turned up as an uninvited visitor at the house. Michael peels a pear and makes a meal. Eve kisses the woman. The family scene is haunted, as many of Smith's are, by companionable lesbians, gentle erotic possibilities. Putting a brick through the glass of marriage no longer seems quite the thing. Family provides in the end what Michael imagines as a *sky of kindness*. He's willing to wait and care for the kids when Eve goes off to America in search of something more.

Yet the problem of who will write about that benign marriage is not entirely resolved, not here, nor in *The Argonauts*, where Nelson vies gently with Harry and their child for the time art takes. The house that Eve and Michael have chosen in Norfolk has a writer's hut, which seems like a reference to Woolf's having had one in Sussex, and her real practice of retreating to the garden in order to write. Eve's hut is like the one that I have dreamed of at various times and places in the world – the one Hans many times offered to build me, in Baltic forests or in American gardens. Eve's desire to be on holiday with her family while working on her new novel seems reasonable, appropriate to twenty-first-century life. But in fact Eve spends her days lying on the floor of the shed smoking cigarettes and despairing of writing anything ever again. The problem is not just spatial, not just economic, not just about history. It's also about audience. What kind of story can the married person tell that does not betray or exclude? What kind of marriage would leave room for me to be talking to you like this? It's not clear at the end of

The Accidental if Eve, who has swerved away from life with Michael and her kids, will write a better novel as a single person or return to writing formulaic ones in her spacious family home in London. Smith leaves it open, while implying that it must be one or the other. Writing about a happy marriage can be harder than living with the infidelities, the plot twists, the interruptions from a stranger, that cause fictional marriages to fail. If Hans and I stay together, what will I write? If you are reading this now, we probably didn't.

CHAPTER FOUR

ORDINARY ADULTERY

That long night on the runway, it did feel that I might just be carrying on an affair. Perhaps Shannon and Hans and I would all eat dinner together and get along fine under our own *sky of kindness*. Before getting on the plane to New York, I'd asked Hans to consider the dubious claim he'd once made that none of our infidelity in the early years of us being together had done us any harm as a couple. We'd had a pretty good talk about that hypothesis over a bottle of sparkling wine. While making love later that night, I'd felt the thrill of life in Brighton and Princeton, everything liberating and new, a kind of conversation between us that was truly original. My love for him bloomed under those conditions of honesty, his traits of willingness and curiosity giving rise to mine. But if this was all the conversation with Shannon was – an ordinary affair – then the problems of narrating it were not solved.

In that era of my own parents' amicable separation I had acquired the idea that a marriage could accommodate many loves. One day in 1983 my friend Milly and I gathered a pile of lemons that had fallen onto her trampoline and made pulpy lemonade, taking it out in a big plastic jug to the street. Milly's mother came in her home-made overalls and gave us a box of paperbacks to sell too, a jumble of things on yoga and tarot-reading, and the 1973 bestseller *Open Marriage*. While we waited for our customers, we read: *the idea of sexually exclusive monogamy breeds deep-rooted dependencies, infantile and childish emotions, and insecurities.* Jealousy is like a *cancer*, wrote the authors; marriage a sickness that needs treatment. Sipping the lemonade, which we'd deliberately made sweet, Milly told me about a man who wrote her mother love poems, which her father pinned to the fridge. This helped to explain why my fashionable aunt, who came from England to visit, with her jeans and Princess Diana haircut, talked only of having boyfriends who were married to other people. And why my parents' friend was intriguingly sad about the death of her lover, even though her husband was still so well and alive.

Before my mother and father officially broke up, my mother began an affair with a man from their group of friends in Adelaide, a bearded philosopher who wore leather trousers complicated by zips and had himself been in an open relationship with an attractive feminist artist. I was too young to understand the details, but my father told me later about an evening he and the philosopher and my mother had spent discussing how the affair should go. My father's pleasure in that scenario came out in his telling of the story. A lifelong contrarian, he took intense pride in his capacity to be infinitely tolerant and playful about a situation that he should in conventional terms have found hard. I imagined the three of them drinking wine under the light of a home-made papier-mâché lampshade, deciding where everyone should go off to sleep, my father being supportive of things continuing just like that. I felt great warmth imagining my father like this, a sense of kinship with him that I often lacked.

I am pretty sure that married people have had sex with people other than their spouses for as long as they have been promising not to. Not all of them, and not always, but consistently more than we talk about. Like sex between men, or between women, I'll bet that the fact of adultery has been drearily consistent across time. The thing that changes is if and how we name it. It's in the speaking that we create a history for all these acts that would otherwise remain ineffably material. That scene of my parents talking about polygamy interests me more than what they did, and it's against their style of 1970s conversation that I measure up my own ability to write about all of this. Novels appear in that light less as evidence of extramarital sex that has or hasn't happened, less as *what we really did*, and more as a sign that sex can at any time shift from being something that merely happens to being something celebrated; from being a quiet fact of survival to being a scene of the desiring self's breaking open against the rocks of social expectation.

In 1979 the literary scholar Tony Tanner published *Adultery in the Novel*, an academic argument for infidelity having been the real lynchpin for the nineteenth-century novel. His close reading of three canonical European novels, *Madame Bovary*, *Elective Affinities* and *Julie; or, the New Eloise*, argues that it is adultery, not marriage, that structures these classics. Fiction depends on the idea that laws exist and get broken. In Goethe's *Elective Affinities* and Rousseau's *Julie*, the extramarital sex doesn't even have to happen: the mere thought of it propels the characters towards death. This might seem like a fairly old-fashioned point for Tanner to be making at a time when *Open Marriage* sat on family bookshelves. But there is a part of his argument that engages directly with the fate of the novel under late twentieth-century conditions. Good plots where married people rebel depend, Tanner argues, on fidelity mattering in the first place. Novels of casual betrayal and pleasure may be realistic, but they are also the end of fiction as we know it.

There is a Danish version of this argument in Suzanne Brøgger's famous 1973 essays, *Deliver Us from Love*. Brøgger is passionately opposed to marriage, but she reconstructs a debate from the press in which a pastor damns the *modern broad-mindedness* of a society where couples separate amicably, socialise together with their new lovers, drink coffee to discuss old times. Danish society can still feel a bit like this: tolerant and liberal towards its people and their foibles. The problem, in this Lutheran pastor's eyes, though, is that modern couples so openly making and breaking vows leave nothing to care or talk about. Almost anything would be better, argues the pastor, than tolerance. Even the actions of a young man from Jutland, who shoots his wife in order to avoid seeing her in the arms of another man, are better than those who keep on drinking tea with their ex-spouses. Tanner is less interested than the pastor in what people actually do. In his own way, he accepts that the *modern broad-mindedness* of the 1970s is a social reality. But both argue that once adultery stops mattering – once men in the provinces no longer shoot their unfaithful wives – good novels get harder to write. It's the loss of plot rather than the immorality that worries them.

I do not know today if Tanner's fears were really warranted. Half a century later, people are still promising fidelity and still breaking their vows, still writing novels about that as if it were noteworthy and surprising. In *An American Marriage*, when Roy is released from prison he re-enters Celeste's life when things between them are impossibly eroded by time and pain. Opening the door to the house they once shared with his old key, Roy returns to a home that is no longer his. Celeste, who has stopped responding to his letters, is now together with the neighbour. But as her husband, Roy reasserts briefly his hold over her body: *when I touch you, your flesh communicates with my bones*. Marriage still seems a relation of immense power, an institution hard to let go of. Adultery in this light is still something to fear, something about which a story can be told.

Perhaps the thing Tanner couldn't have foreseen is that new versions of adultery would become hard to talk about for new reasons. Now that the old incentives to get married (for money, for social approval, for a child, so someone will cook dinner) have mostly dried up, it's a little embarrassing to find that adultery has remained part of the routine. With the promises that we make as queer and quirky as we can write, it's hard to explain how breaking them could still happen. For a long time marriage was a perfectly respectable cover for all kinds of forbidden love: for queer sex, or an affair with someone of the wrong class. Once at a London playground I met a man, a fellow parent, who told me that he was married to another man, who had started having an affair. Searching for an appropriate response, I told him about an eighteenth-century duchess who brought up her husband's illegitimate daughter while living with her best friend, a divorcee who became her husband's lover. She then fell in love and had a child with someone else, all under the roof of that high-society marriage. I could have talked about Lowell, his crushes on other women being a regular part of his life with Hardwick. Or about the suburbs of the 1950s. Before the days of contraception and no-fault divorce, the best lesbian affairs flourished between wives who felt no pressure to leave or to make a big deal of the things they got up to, after the breakfast dishes were done. Talking through the bars of the climbing frame while our kids threw themselves on the squidgy ground, I could have invoked hundreds of historical scenarios that once made sense of married couples having other lovers. But with financial independence and shared custody and gay marriage all possible, none of these old arrangements seem any longer quite defensible. *I guess we'll just end it*, said the father, zipping his son's coat closed against the cold.

If loving Shannon was not a drama leading somewhere – not a true secret, not a way of discovering myself, not a reason for Hans to load his gun, not a great injury to anyone or an offence to society – it was probably not something to write or talk about. Grindr and the dark web, our modern versions of screwing the servant casually while your wife waits upstairs for her tea, or nurturing a thing for women that it is impossible to speak about with your husband, are hardly topics for playground conversation. But the good affair – the one that makes you feel happy while turning your life into something that faces in two directions – that's also become difficult to justify as anything but a new story entirely.

*

The spring before I met Shannon, I spent two weeks alone in Leamington Spa. I wouldn't normally have stayed that long in England, with the kids in Copenhagen, but it was exam time and there was a long stint of marking and invigilation to do. Borrowing a colleague's flat, a small place with a plush fold-out sofa and books stored for times of teaching, I stayed alone, feeling the quiet pleasure of not having to take care of anyone except myself. The kitchen ran dry of everything but coffee beans. I wrote slow emails and notes on the papers of my students. When I was too tired to work, I switched on the lamp and pulled down Sally Rooney's *Conversations with Friends* from the shelf. I knew it as a novel Marie had read when it came out in 2017, remembered buying it for her on the recommendation of the enthusiastic young saleswoman at Waterstones.

Back then, aged fifteen, Marie had told me keenly about Rooney's protagonists, Bobbi and Frances, students in Dublin with their low intake of calories and high output of text and electronic communication. The novel seemed in her rendition to be confessional, but not in a way that told everything. I was curious about the affair between Bobbi and Frances, students and poets who had supposedly been lovers before the time of the novel began. Marie explained that the affair was left largely to the imagination, but *plausibly*, she insisted, insinuating that all her female friends might once have been lovers now. I was pretty sure she couldn't imagine that being the case, not as anything specifically to do with fingers or tongues. But at that time neither could I. The confusing thing, in Marie's rendition of Rooney's story, was that it seemed also to be about Frances getting together with

Nick. *Rooney's characters are like us*, said Marie, invoking a group of friends with secrets, long hair, the propensity to betray each other for the love of older men.

Lying back on the sofa as the evening fell quiet and early over that Victorian spa town, I wondered what Marie, now sixteen, was doing in Copenhagen. *Conversations with Friends* was still being feted, but I felt late to the party. Or perhaps it was just that the novel's whole tone suggests there was a before time, when everyone was younger and could get away with things better. Frances is very young when she falls in love with Nick, the actor, who is married to Melissa, the photojournalist, and has afternoons and nights of sex with him kept secret from both Melissa and her friend and ex-lover, Bobbi. Frances records her abjection about all this, noting Nick's softness around the edges, his fondness for babies and dogs, his agility at shopping for groceries on command, from the point of view of a student in a shared flat. Later in the novel, their affair becomes open.

In Leamington Spa I reached this turning point in the novel as my hunger grew. With the fridge empty, I wondered if I should stop reading and go and buy food from the Waitrose down the road. But I could not abandon Frances, weak with period pain, lying in the bath while Nick watches her kindly, not objectifying her. She steps out of the water, he wraps a towel around her, Bobbi strums a ukulele in her room, everything is peaceful in the aftermath of her pain. In this setting, Nick reveals to Frances that he's told his wife about their affair:

> I spoke to Melissa, he said. I told her we've been seeing each other. Is that OK?

I closed my eyes. What happened? I asked quietly.

We talked for a while. I think she's all right. I told her that I wanted to keep seeing you and she understands that, so.

This is not an adultery scene of the kind Tanner imagines – illegitimate desire challenging the whole bourgeois order and bringing the novel to life. It's not *Anna Karenina*, either, where the perfectly fine husband wouldn't have minded Anna's affair so much if the whole world didn't have to know about it. I still had a good chunk of *Conversations with Friends* to go. With everything out in the open, the spaces of agonised reflection and intimacy legitimate, the ukulele in the background, Frances's story kept on going in that deliberately casual style of youthful narration.

Marie called to say hello. I told her I was reading *Conversations with Friends. Frances wasn't very credibly queer*, I said. *It seems like she might rather just be married to Nick and not having all this complicated experience.* Marie explained I was missing the whole point of Frances being difficult and contradictory – *I was a professor of novels and should know that Rooney was more critical of her character than that.* Marie was at home studying for a debate. *I have no time to read novels now*, she said. She told me I *should try reading Thomas Piketty.* We hung up and I went back to *Conversations with Friends.* The subjectivity of Rooney, like that of Marie, seemed in some way new and triumphant. But if any generation could claim to have promoted polygamy, or introduced new levels of transparency and kindness around sex, I didn't think it was theirs. I wanted the praise

Conversations with Friends had won as a story about sex to flow backwards in time, for credit to go to my parents and their friends for having had the courage to actually try and live like that after they grew up.

Conversations with Friends made me think in comparison of Margaret Drabble's 1969 novel *The Waterfall*. Beginning in the third person, it tells of a winter night in London when Jane has just given birth to her second child in a shabby but somewhat valuable house in London. The midwife has left and so has Jane's husband, a classical guitarist whose professional star is on the rise. Jane and the baby are being cared for by her cousin Lucy, and by Lucy's kind and desirable husband, James. Snow falls, days and nights pass, James and Lucy come and take shifts reading at her bedside, changing the sheets, making the tea. James is the better nurse. More than most characters, he loves babies: he's wanted Lucy to have more than three. The scene where he helps Jane to recover in the overheated bedroom, a palpable hothouse of milk and blood, seems as extraordinary now as when I puzzled over it as a teenager. Could a man desire a woman who had just given birth to someone else's child? The possibility registered for me as the premonition of adulthood in all its complexity, a sip straight from a bottle of Scotch.

James plumps the pillow, reads a book, blends into the warmth of the room in a mood of identification as well as desire. It feels as if he would willingly nurse the baby himself. He enters Jane's bed long before they make love, staying there intermittently over the next months while she cares for the kids, faces the world as a single mother, gets the all-clear from the doctor to have sex again. Lovemaking relies on Jane staying awake after sleepless nights with the children, but it is earth-shattering and lovely, more convincing perhaps than the exploratory, slightly forensic sex between Nick and Frances in *Conversations with Friends*. Orgasms contribute palpably to Jane finding the first-person voice in which she delivers up parts of the novel, and in which she apologises for, excuses and finally owns her adultery as being not so bad. *Not the worst thing in the world.*

As a story of sex sustaining a woman in distress, *The Waterfall* holds up well next to *Conversation with Friends*. It is quirkier and more attentive to the way people having affairs must also move through space and time along with children, their toys, mothers, dying house plants. Was Drabble's version of adultery newer in 1969 than Rooney's in 2017? When Lucy finds out about her husband's affair with her cousin, she and Jane get drunk in a hotel room while their kids, who are all cousins, are sleeping. Lucy says more or less that Jane is welcome to him. But in fact James and Lucy's marriage hardly wavers in the end. Jane observes their resilience as a couple with slight envy, while discovering that she's actually the lucky one. The affair between Jane and James continues openly, with Jane renovating her house and publishing a book of intimate poems about James. He objects only slightly to the disclosure. The novel ends with the adulterous couple on a holiday together in a bed-and-breakfast while Jane's children are with their grandparents.

I was thinking about Marie again that night in early 2019 when the plane was stuck on the runway in the snow. In the months since we'd talked on the phone about Rooney, I had met Shannon. I had not told her much, only snippets describing a gender-queer person I liked so much. She pounced on these smartly. *Are you two having an affair?* Before that trip to New York, I could with some impunity say *no*. But I knew how much she would like Shannon, and I was loath to repel her curiosity entirely. Thinking back to her enthusiasm about Rooney, I wondered what Marie's feelings about this real adultery would be. Despite her open-mindedness about everything queer, I doubted she'd approve of what I was doing that night – flying around the world to have sex with someone I had been writing to for months.

In Tanner's diagnosis, the traditional novel pits the longing self against the social contracts that bind everything together. That conflict drives the story, the need to be with the person you love competing with society's need for you to care for your kids and keep your family together. If it had been easy for Julie or Anna Karenina or the Princesse de Clèves to get everything they wanted, their stories would have been raunchy tales of sex held together by language alone. Tanner points to John Updike's fiction as an example of what happens when narrative is deprived of the tensions of morality. He might have been thinking of *Couples*, a 1968 novel full of high-octane descriptions of the swinging scene in the American suburbs. There are few moral dilemmas there, just plenty of semen smeared across the furniture. If Tanner had read Drabble or Baldwin or Highsmith, or even Rooney or Jenny Offill or Junot Díaz today, he might have been more optimistic about adultery remaining a creative problem. Or he might have feared even more intensely the post-1970 novel becoming a vehicle for selves and their nothingness, a chorus of narcissistic voices so good to listen to that it's hard not to be grateful for the betrayals of which they speak.

In the decade that Salter's *Light Years* tracks most closely, Viri desperately desires and eventually sleeps with his secretary. The secret leaves him racked with desire as well as a nauseating fear of exposure. Nedra's trysts are less secret and therefore more subject to scrutiny by Viri. Her most significant affair is with Jivan, who becomes a regular at the family table, driving up in his furniture-removal van and quietly claiming his place there. Later, Nedra takes a new lover, Andre:

> When Viri mentioned Andre, whose presence was just beginning to be felt, who did not yet leave telephone messages or sit at their table, Nedra calmly replied that she found him interesting.
>   They were alone in the kitchen. Autumn filled the air.
>   'Just how interesting?'
>   'Oh, Viri, you know.'
>   'As interesting as Jivan?'
>   'No,' she said. 'To be honest, no.'
>   'I wish I didn't find it so disturbing.'
>   'It's not that important,' she said.
>   'These things ... I'm sure you realize these things, done openly ...'
>   'Yes?'
>   'Can have a profound effect upon children.'

Nedra is the one who makes the bed in *Light Years* and gets described as sexy. She's also the one who leaves Viri in the end, driven by a wish to travel and grow. She tells him on a long-planned trip to London that she's not coming home.

Light Years reminds me of my mother's desire in the late 1970s for movement, community, affairs. Already, as her girl-child, I understood her right to these things. The logic of second-wave feminism ran between the pages of the books she owned: the Drabble, the *Joy of Sex*, *The Women's Room*, *The Female Eunuch*. Even Salter's mostly sympathetic account of Nedra's affairs suggests the spirit of male self-assertion that my mother was facing down. Viri keeps his adultery secret, but walks away from Nedra when she argues: *but isn't it better to be someone who follows her true life and is happy and generous, than an embittered woman who is loyal? Isn't that so?* In that conversation I hear a whole chorus of women discovering happiness as the only thing a feminist can really be faithful to. A generation later, Hans and I were happy making those homes successively in Vancouver and Ann Arbor and Copenhagen. Our slight betrayals were more equally distributed. There was none of the obvious inequality that Nedra fled from. But it was daunting after Marie was born, and Rohan eight years later, to find ourselves so deeply obliged to each other for childcare, so far flung apart as people who only got to really be out in the world when the other was at home with the kids. One of us was often at an academic conference, sleeping in a hotel in a place like Pittsburgh, Cleveland, St Louis or Southampton, while the other was back in Vancouver or Ann Arbor making breakfast and folding the laundry. Somewhere in that stew of frequent flight, books we feared we'd never find time to write, weeks going by without either of us having time for sex with each other or alone, I had affairs. They were mostly unremarkable, sweet and storyless, as Tanner feared – afternoons in bed filled up with conversation that drifted towards discussions of children and work. A transcript of that pillow-talk would have sounded like we were colleagues talking over a bottle of wine. Once or twice, like Nedra, I brought a lover back to our house and he played with my kids, sat around our table in an ordinary way. I am telling this as an illustration of Tanner's point, that routine adultery might be the end of the novel, rather than as a confession of wrongdoing.

Yet Tanner forgets that some novels actually honour this enlarged, maybe even robust definition of family life that part of me wanted adultery to lead to. Fictional scenes crisscrossed with polyamory may be unsatisfying in narrative terms, but they sometimes become the scenes of a domesticity most recognisable to me as ideal. What would have happened in *Another Country* if Ida had invited that boy on the landing in? Vivaldo sleeps in the end with Eric, leaving it unlikely but possible that Eric will come over for dinner with him and Ida in the future. Even *Amelia*, with its promotion of the happy marriage, doesn't oppose it entirely to the adultery that sets its story going. As the novel opens, Booth finds himself locked up with an ex-lover in a debtors' prison, telling stories and having the kind of sex that makes the time pass quickly. Booth tries unsuccessfully to conceal the affair when he returns to his family. But it's an issue of practical discomfort rather than moral conflict; in other ways, it's proof that Booth and Amelia both remain attractive beings, magnets for the admirers they bring home and the good kinds of sociability this supports.

Amelia is a first attempt at something that has remained difficult to write: a novel that promotes as its ethical horizon a manifold and complicated version of commitment in which loves are many, and adultery is present but not the key ethical dilemma. Perhaps this describes Boris Pasternak's Russian classic of the 1950s, *Doctor Zhivago*, whose protagonist loves Lara as well as his good wife, Tonja. When he is imprisoned by the rebel army, Zhivago finds his way back to both women, burying his skis at the foot of a rowan tree in the forest, whose berries are the last source of food for the birds in the winter. He imagines that tree yielding nutrients like some great wet nurse, unbuttoning herself, tutting as she lets them feed on her orange fruit. The tree becomes emblematic in his mind of a polyamorous state of love. Pulling at its branches, Zhivago feels Lara stretching out her strong, snowy arms to meet him. With its fruit let down into the community of the needy, the tree's care flows freely along multiple and unusual tributaries, from Lara and Zhivago towards their spouses, towards children not their own, towards each other.

Pasternak – like Drabble, like Salter – tries out that radical conjecture: the idea that adultery and familial love might not be in competition. Once Zhivago finds Lara again, he learns that she has helped Tonja give birth, and that Tonja has returned with the children to Moscow. Unable to follow, and in danger of persecution, Zhivago heads out with Lara to the abandoned estate where his and Tonja's child was conceived the previous winter. The snow is deep, and

Lara herself is now pregnant with Zhivago's child. But the child who is with them, Katenka, is not his. Her father is the revolutionary leader Strelnikov, the novel's other hero. In bed with Zhivago, Lara admits that under the right circumstances, if a house appeared in which he sat at his desk by lamplight, she would crawl back to Strelnikov on her knees. By any account, the network of loyalties and duties involved here is complex. But Zhivago plays joyfully with Katenka on the sled and, when he watches her and Lara sleeping in the frozen estate, he is conscious only of a simple wave of love uniting them all.

The Waterfall also strains actively towards the idea that an adulterous parent might be a good one. Scenes where James helps to look after Jane's children, engaging them with tenderness practised on his own, actively present that possibility. As they fall into that larger muddle of care, Jane suggests that the true parents of any baby are those who treat it with love. *The Waterfall* probes that contention, throws down adultery's gauntlet bravely in the way of paternity. In *Light Years*, Jivan says he loves Nedra and Viri's daughters. The kids are happiest in his presence. On Christmas Eve, Jivan comes to the family house, lights the fire and listens with special care when the children speak. Franca, the oldest, registers the quality of her mother's lover's attention towards her being warmer and more festive than her father's.

I approved of my mother's affair with the philosopher. He was a rogue figure who brought me books in the saddlebag of his motorbike and talked to me as someone who would grow up to understand them. He was also the father of my friend Jonah, whose disregard for rules I admired, and whose

mother was a feminist famous for her screen-prints and
public art. During that year when the philosopher was seeing
my mother, he took me and Jonah camping. We drove out
in his open-sided jeep to a national park, stopping to look
at snakes and animal skeletons, jolting along without shoes
or seatbelts. The philosopher seemed to me a conquering
hero of that landscape. He kept his tent pitched on a finger
of sand, along with a barrel for collecting rainwater, a heavy
black pot over a firepit, and a tin chest full of canned food
buried like pirates' treasure. I relished the idea that our lives
were illegitimately entangled. Regardless of what was happening with me and Hans, there was something intensely
moving to me in the idea of Shannon knowing and loving
my kids.

And yet the adulterer's plight is never easy, the temptation
it brings to break a life into two parts always strong. Novels
show this split life as having both its costs and its advantages.
At one point in *Light Years*, Viri tries to convince himself
that a secret affair is perfectly natural. Secrecy is what defines
him as he picks at his lust for Kaya, the secretary, with whom
he is having an affair that Salter describes as a wound. Later,
when Nedra is asked to describe the life she has lived, she asks
herself: *Which one?* It's been hard for her morally, in the face
of Viri's incriminations, and as a mother, to defend her love
affairs. For the purposes of telling a story, having two lives
might have been easier. It's the kind of structure that Tanner
has in mind when he pays tribute to the novel as the effect of
incommensurate desires and strictures. Having a place from
which to reflect on another is a technical boon. The world

you share with your wife, which you talk about with your lover. Or: the life you had with your spouse before you knew about her adultery, followed by the one you have afterwards, when everything unravels as a story told to a stranger.

This is the premise of Ford Madox Ford's *The Good Soldier*. Long before I recognised that novel as a feat of narration or understood why it had been assigned to me in a course, it intrigued me. The copy I have on my shelves right now is inked through like an old bandage, its passages underlined in reddish-brown pen, its pages drifting out of alignment. My marks grow bloodiest in passages where Dowell, the narrator, appears. They define the novel's frame narrative, which takes place in a cottage in the dark, beside a fire. Rain is beating on the windows and Dowell is telling what he describes as the saddest story we will ever hear. This is the imagined scene of delivery for *The Good Soldier*. The next frame down involves Dowell, a rich American, having a conversation in which he is forcibly enlightened by his English friend, Leonora, about the fact that her husband, Edward, and Dowell's wife, Flora, were lovers. The affair has spread over many years as the two couples sojourn together in the spas and sanatoriums of Europe. Dowell learns the truth in Leonora's country house in England, once Flora is dead.

As my markings show, I was always invested in Dowell. But Dowell is a shadowy figure, barely substantiated physically, held together mostly by a will not to know anything of the debauchery and predation that has unfolded around him. He has overlooked – or claims to have overlooked – the fact that Flora married him in the first place in order to provide cover for her affair with another man. Her heart condition, which barred him from her bedroom, was a thin fabrication. Dowell has also failed to see all the evidence pointing to the fact that Edward, his best friend, is a tortured man whose serial adulteries bankrupted and enraged Leonora. Dowell claims ignorance of it all, as well as of his own sublimated love for Nancy, Leonora and Edward's adopted daughter.

The Good Soldier seems less concerned with the truth of any of these relations than with finding out what moral purpose revealing them could serve. Having spent ten years in a state of oblivion to the affairs of those around him, Dowell is the last, unwilling keeper of those stories. The only character more naïve than him about love and sex has been Nancy. Of adultery, she knows that she's commanded not to commit it. *But why, she thought, should one? It was probably something like catching salmon out of season – a thing one did not do. She gathered it had something to do with kissing, or holding someone in your arms.* When Nancy is forced by Leonora to recognise that she has been the object of both Edward and Dowell's desire, the levelling up in understanding, and the sense of her own role in those adult dramas, drives her insane. On the rainy night on which Dowell is describing all this to us, Nancy sits half mad in an adjacent room.

Dowell, on the other hand, stays sane by passing minimal judgement. He assumes the rank of the one who knows the most with only the quietest of nods to the virtue of revelation. Society, he supposes, depends on the flourishing of the slightly deceitful. Those who are too truthful are condemned to suicide and insanity. So which side of this equation is Ford on? Dowell expresses a strong preference for facts remaining hidden, and yet he is here telling us everything. And we are here reading the things that adulterers normally would not tell, getting all the details that repression or deceit could have saved us from. The whole elegant premise of the novel is that telling involves as much violence as infidelity itself. It's the relation of the unsaid to the said that keeps society together, more than obedience to the law.

When I told Hans about Shannon, he was not scandalised, not even hurt at first. We had enough evidence from our early days that transgression could be reabsorbed into our intimacy. The fact that we were older now, and that Shannon was living on the other side of the Atlantic, could have made it all perfectly sustainable. The problem that autumn was that I was already telling Shannon so many things that I wasn't telling Hans. Our online conversations had ballooned to a scale that Hans and I could not compete with, especially while we were also living and working and parenting together. Sometimes having one life in which to do all the fucking and the arguing and the parenting doesn't leave much room for narration. The therapist we spent precious time with when the kids were at school thought that perhaps I'd been too quick to confess to the affair in the first place. Her office was in an old warehouse near the beach, an area dotted with brick-walled cafés. An amber pendant hung in the folds of her well-draped clothes. *Sometimes a don't ask, don't tell policy is helpful,* she suggested brightly. Clearly she saw us as people with too many words at our disposal, lacking the proper desire to hide things from each other.

As a teacher of American freshmen, I used sometimes to write three questions on the board: *Who Is Speaking? To*

Whom? For What Purpose? These are good questions to ask of almost any narrator as well as of someone confessing to adultery. In a world where it has become easier in certain ways to talk about this stuff, at least if it is framed in the context of youth and experimentation, it's not always clear what the point of telling is. When the therapist suggested that I was perhaps *just not into men*, I said all kind of things about how besotted with masculinity Shannon had made me. But to whom could I say that properly, if not to Shannon? Wasn't the real point that she was becoming the one I wanted to confess to, rather than the one I wanted to talk about?

When Simone de Beauvoir's letters to Jean-Paul Sartre were first published in 1990, many readers were scandalised by how she described, for Sartre's benefit, the sex she had with other people. This was the twentieth century's most famous feminist philosopher serving up her own experiences for a man's pleasure. She narrated for him her affair with Jacques-Laurent Bost, a man whom she and Sartre both liked. In July 1938 Beauvoir wrote from a walking trip in the Alps to tell Sartre that she and Bost had ended up sleeping together in a barn where they'd stopped overnight: *we spend*, she writes, *idyllic days, and nights of passion*. She goes on to stress that Sartre shouldn't fear that she will be out of sorts or disorientated when they meet the next weekend. The affair with Bost is light and agreeable, *but it has its proper place in my life*. A year later, with Bost and Sartre both stationed away from Paris, Beauvoir corresponds almost daily with each of them, relaying news of one to the other, encouraging them to share books.

At around this time Beauvoir also started sleeping with women. To Sartre, in October 1939 she reports:

... Sorkine turned up and, as in the month of July, pulled me first onto the bed, then – amidst sobs – into her arms and towards her mouth; finally, after about an hour, she even drew my hand to specific parts of her body. After this she was nervous and mistrustful, rummaging in my bag and wanting to take my diary. She's the very image of 'unripe fruit' – with movements of agreeable, floating tenderness, but at other times the convulsive movements of an adolescent girl at the awkward age. She told me lots of sweet nothings in Russian, and once in French: 'I love you so! – I love you so much, so much!

This is just one description of the many encounters squeezed into days when Beauvoir teaches, keeps her diary, updates Bost and Sartre on her feelings and has enough sex to supply her letters with their content. Many of the letters are written in cafés, with lovers waiting in the wings, ready to confront her on the pavement, flirt with her from the next table. Telling casts its own kind of spell over events that are still unfolding. There is nothing to be done: here I am, caught up in an affair, *in media res*. The really shocking thing about what Sartre and Beauvoir were doing is that live streaming of their acts. Real-time confessions, as I was learning in my own letters to Shannon, can feel more pornographic than those that come after the fact.

Ford Madox Ford, author of *The Good Soldier*, changed his name in order to avoid the scandal of association with his first wife, a Catholic who refused to divorce him. His lives with subsequent lovers, women with whom he set up cottages in the country, printing presses, artistic endeavours, were overshadowed by the scandal of that first wife's insistence that he could not un-marry or forget her. Ford's portrait of Edward – each of his passionate Catholic attachments eclipsing the last, each getting a firm hold on his imagination, with no one to tell it all to properly – is not entirely beyond the pale. Ford led his own life as a serial monogamist, subscribing fully to each possibility of romantic renewal. Spread out in time, his affairs can seem moral unto themselves, if difficult to see that way in sequence or from the perspective of the estranged wife. But there was only one person hearing each part of his story. Adultery is not simply a matter of culture and of history, but also of how we choose to space it out and relate it over time.

I've assumed it's best not to leave behind a life riven in two, a thing to be pieced together by those who come after. I do not want this life I've led being a thing of speculation. I hate the idea that someone could stumble into Shannon's archives and find it full of letters from me – claim this as an affair to be discovered. I remember my mother announcing to my brothers and stepsisters that she was going to keep a diary and leave it out in a place where anyone who wanted could read it. *A kind of public history, proof that her feelings were nothing to hide.* The announcement made me feel shame about the times I'd pried into her life. Surely, I thought, she had every right to keep a diary secretly. Yet the awkwardly open diary put her on the side of the famous female adulterers who have asserted their right to do openly what men have done in secret for so long. Beauvoir has gone down in history for insisting that we do not have to accept our biological destiny. Thank God we are not fish or monkeys, and that we have our menstrual cycles in command. Her many affairs, and her pride in them, follow on from this logic, expending her greed for a life larger than the one that is biologically given. Anna and Emma and Lara and Nedra and Jane form a small army of women insisting on more, holding up their bowls for a refill, putting it all down on paper in their own words before anyone else can. Their sexual transgressions may not be the best expressions of freedom perhaps, but nor are they the worst things in the world. I am writing this now – a version of the diary that my mother gave up after a short while – in solidarity with them wanting more in the right way; in the belief that the good affair is something that should be carried and told rather than hidden away.

CHAPTER FIVE

THE CLIMAX

It was after midnight when the runway cleared and the passengers spilled at last from the plane out into the empty airport. There was a wait at immigration, a moment in Shannon's arms, a short drive under orange airport lights. Buttons must have been pressed, my bag carried, my teeth brushed. We must have done all those things and must even have found words for what we were doing. But the thing I recall more clearly is looking up as the dawn was breaking and feeling the words from *Monkey Grip*, the novel that had initiated me into realism, spinning towards me across the room of the airport hotel. Nora and Javo have retreated to a bunkbed while the kids are out playing in the yard. *I seemed to start coming immediately*, writes Nora; *he saw it and smiled with joy, and we came together effortlessly, smiling and smiling into each other's faces.* The words were so banal, a child's horn sounding the way for sex so nice it might justify being with or becoming a junkie. I hadn't read them since I was nine and it seemed improbable I'd remembered them. Later I looked them up to confirm that I had them right.

Early critics of the novel thought all readers of fiction knew too much about sex. The general disapprobation of reading fixated on the fiddlehead body curled up or around itself, schoolboys with dirty magazines, girls with romances and their hands between their legs. Jane Eyre hidden after a fight behind the curtains of a window seat, armed with an illustrated book about birds. She is not reading about sex, but she is caught up in an action of pleasure taken alone, hidden behind drapes. This might be the way Brontë imagines her own reader reading, even if her material is not directly erotic. For centuries people feared the way books inflamed desire. Do not let your daughters read too much or they will end up wanting more and more – more satisfaction and understanding and pleasure than a properly matched husband can give. They will begin touching themselves or each other. Eve Kosofsky Sedgwick, well known for writings judiciously peppered with personal example, describes days of her childhood spent in autoerotic reverie in her room, her activity half registered by her family. This arrangement, she argues in an essay famously entitled 'Jane Austen and the Masturbating Girl', has structured the casting of female characters and their readers as bodies in need of salvation from their own imagination, while tacitly acknowledging the ability of their fingers to match it.

There's little to fear from the novel on this front these days. Almost everything there is to know about the technicalities of sex can be called up on any screen. It's hard to think of the acts spelled out in *Fanny Hill* or *Lady Chatterley's Lover* as scandalous when there's so much pixelated evidence of all the things people really like and want. But even in my childhood it wasn't fiction that taught me what lovers could actually do: it was *The Joy of Sex*, which I read by studying the drawings laid out intriguingly across the foolscap pages, following limbs and beards that disappeared into the crack of the well-read book. All those invectives against leather, and in favour of denim and open marriage and massage. Long before I experienced anything like desire, I absorbed that version of 1970s advice about the healthy pleasures of breakfast in bed, body hair, fetishes and feathers.

What I got from novels was a more complex idea of sex as something symbolic, something that stood in a vital way for love. Nora and Javo's bunkbed union was just the tip of the iceberg when it came to that kind of intimacy – an act expressing deep compatibility, the unlikely but possible prospect of them working it out and staying together. The sex I learned about in novels was applied as the ultimate proof of concept: the *seal* on love, as Ella puts in Doris Lessing's *The Golden Notebook*. In these terms, the better the sex one is having with someone, the firmer that seal sits, and the stronger the love must be. My mother liked Lessing and sometimes tried rewinding this logic too: *the stronger the love is*, she suggested to me when I was a teenager inclined against love, *the firmer the seal sets, the better the sex will be*. For a while every story I read about sex seemed to abide by that equation.

It was tempting to have that equivalence in mind as Shannon and I drove away from Newark the next morning, besotted and unslept. *I am so happy*, I sang to the planes coming in to land and to the tall New Jersey furnaces burning against the polluted sky. As she drove, Shannon nodded to a bright-pink book sitting on the dashboard of her car, a compilation of stories from women who'd become lesbians after forty. She said she'd bought it for me as a present the day before when she'd been with a friend in an LGBTQ bookshop. *It's a joke*, she said: *you don't have to read it*. But I opened it that evening in the room of the hotel where we stopped. I lay in the crumpled bed, skimming the accounts of married women surprised by the pleasure of getting naked with their friends. The story of Tori playing with Barbara in the spa leaves no doubt about it: if a woman's toe turns you on more than your husband's body, you should certainly sleep with her. If doing it makes you want to explode with happiness, then the whole moral arc of the new universe bends towards that outcome.

The same alignment, the body and mind and heart all pointing in the same direction, drives Carol and Therese out along the road and into each other's arms in *The Price of Salt*. By this logic of good sex, a woman's body is a divining rod that can be used in pursuit of truth. I heard Nedra shouting across the decades at Viri. I also heard the authors of *The Lesbian Joy of Sex*, published only a few years after the straight version, insisting in chorus that the things women want are so wholesome, so fun, so reciprocal, that wanting them must be right: no leather, no whips, just denim grinding happily on denim. That tautology had migrated during my lifetime from the arena of feminism to the ideas circulating about queer sex. Where sex suggests pleasure, the pleasure it suggests is good and real. The logic sheltered me on our road trip like a low-hanging branch, harvested for decades by writers I knew. But even if this tree had produced plenty of fruit for those who needed it, deep down I suspected that I had little right to that whole *seal*-on-love kind of argument. Hadn't I had plenty of good sex with people I did not love – plenty of sex that was not true?

When I thought about it more, that whole equation seemed to support a certain kind of fictional scenario better than the real ones I'd known. There is no obvious sex in *Wuthering Heights, Jane Eyre* or *Pride and Prejudice*. But there are plenty of relationships in those novels that need legitimation in the way Nora and Javo's does in *Monkey Grip*. We are not meant to speculate closely in the case of Heathcliff and Cathy on who exactly gets pleasure from whom, or how it lines up, or whether good chemistry mitigates other kinds of communicative failure. But these characters and their paper bodies come charged with the power to deliver sex as a vindication of love. Rochester may grip Jane's arm harder than he should, but the fact that she does not run away from him and those large dogs, that brooding lust, suggests all will be well when they finally get to the bedroom.

The way we imagine sex for these nineteenth-century characters shows up in versions of novels made for film and television, in sex scenes that retrofit those old, unequal partnerships to our modern sense of what sex looks like. In composing such scenes, readers are at liberty to move backwards across time, taking Garner's modern descriptions of Javo's special ways as an infinitely slow lover to help fill in Austen's blanks. Darcy took his time. Elizabeth started coming immediately. Darcy saw it and recognised it, and smiled back at her through the haze of his own pleasure. Rochester didn't really want to hurt Jane: he wanted her, and she wanted him too. These encomiums to mutual pleasure apply to fictional couples and romantic scenarios more easily than to what we actually do in bed.

The pink book in Shannon's car suggested that the whole seal-on-love logic applies best when we know our true object of desire. I would not, in this sense, have been a good subject for that book: I never simply or secretly wanted to sleep with women. I had no feeling of having found myself, at least not in the fact of Shannon being a woman. But I had chafed as a reader, as well as a lover, against certain versions of heterosexual sex. Take that scene in *Monkey Grip* where the definition of good lovemaking depends essentially on timing. Garner uses the climax to anoint the union of the single mother and her drug-addicted lover. That choreography has long been deployed in less interesting contexts to suggest a natural fit between men and women, a locking together of bodies programmed for each other. In *Lady Chatterley's Lover* the well-timed orgasm is more important than any other kind of coincidence. Lawrence decries a woman bringing on her own pleasure after a man has finished. He reads it as a sign of resistance, a woman holding herself back rather than falling into step with a man. Surely, says Connie Chatterley to the hangdog playwright Michaelis, with whom she has lacklustre sex when her husband has gone to bed, *you want me to have my satisfaction too, don't you?* But Michaelis, resentful of the fact that the women he sleeps with fail to reach their climax at his pace, is cruelly honest in his response: *Oh, all right! I'm quite willing. But I'm damned if hanging on waiting for a woman to go off is much of a game for a man.* Connie is genuinely confused, having imagined her own pleasure as something to be shared.

It is only when Connie and the gamekeeper start having simultaneous orgasms that everything else about their relationship begins to make sense. Nothing supplies a vindication of their adultery and class miscegenation like this double act, first accomplished on a pile of wood in the forest while the dog waits patiently, nose to paws. *It's good when it's like that. Most folks live their lives through and never know it,* says Mellors as Connie lies in the forest nest he has made, half dressed in the clothes he has torn open. Connie accepts her own desire being explained back to her. But there are signs of her being less content than Mellors with what has just happened. Her lover's words of praise for their timing leave her wondering about other women he has loved and come off together with. Why doesn't he simply lie down and cover her again with his body?

Objectively Lawrence is progressive, writing in the 1920s of female pleasure as a large part of sex. But he is also quick to shame the woman's body. Her clit becomes a *hungry beak*, a greedy, unlovely thing; her inability to come in unison with a man an act of sullen insurrection. By the 1930s and 40s many manuals for married couples were advocating this same kind of alignment of orgasms that seems radical in Lawrence, prescribing that tricky piece of choreography as the key to holding a marriage in place. That private trajectory helped, as Annamarie Jagose puts it, to inscribe *heterosexuality as the natural expression of time itself.* Moving forward at the same pace, the man and woman who can do this for each other in bed are equipped for all the rhythms of life and reproduction that a marriage can withstand.

It would be claiming too much to say that I sensed what

was conservative about Lawrence's sex scenes at fifteen. *Sons and Lovers* and *Women in Love* enchanted me then with their flowers, dialogues, brightly coloured stockings, coal fires burning in small rooms, the monologues of women angry about their limited place in the world, their description of women's work, the lines of sight revealed as women look at naked men with appreciation and desire. In my days of high-school truancy I studied *Sons and Lovers*, fascinated with the way Miriam's mind is always just out of reach of Paul's. But it is true that those novels – as precious to me as stained-glass windows refracting through their emerald and fuchsia panes the light of impending womanhood – never made me feel desire.

The same goes for Doris Lessing. Her investments in women's happiness are more obvious than Lawrence's. How compellingly she writes in one breath about women's bleeding, about their longing for men who will not leave their wives, about their weight gain and their appetite for political involvement. But on the topic of female pleasure, Lessing is not so different from Lawrence. *The Golden Notebook* was written in 1962 in an era when the Kinsey Report was making it clear that all kinds of sex could be considered good by the different people having it. But the objective language of description in Lessing's love scenes supports only the simplest conventions of intercourse. When Ella and Paul first make love, her orgasms are far better than those he gives her by hand in the demise of their relationship: *Vaginal orgasm that is. And she could not have experienced it if she had not loved him. It is the orgasm that is created by the man's need for a woman, and his confidence in that need.* Not much later, Mary McCarthy's

The Group describes with similar precision Dottie's climax, brought on disappointingly by Dick's thumb: *it left her jumpy and disconcerted, it was something less thrilling and more like being tickled relentlessly or having to go to the bathroom.* It cannot compare to the first one she's had with him inside her.

Lady Chatterley's Lover and *The Golden Notebook* were important books for me. But the sex scenes I choreographed for myself were differently timed, applying what I knew of 1970s soft porn to the characters I loved in far earlier novels. In the juxtaposition of scenes and logics across centuries, I could imagine the early days of marriage when Rochester brought Jane breakfast in bed, letting the cooling tea trickle down her chin and over her nipples before sucking carefully on each one. Or the times when Elizabeth came effortlessly as Darcy applied his hands to her body. Or the times Mr Bennet dressed up as a redcoat for his young wife while she touched herself in pleasure. It was not mutual orgasm I imagined, but the give and take, the criss-crossing of books and ideas and rhythms easy for the historian to miss.

The sex I had with a woman in Brighton that first year Hans was in America wasn't a success. She was a younger student at Sussex. She'd grown up with British parents in a small French town. Imogen had invited her to a party at our flat. We kissed in the kitchen when I asked about her tongue-ring. *I'll show you how it feels*, she offered. Later she asked, first in French, then in English, *can I sleep with you?* I did not know exactly what she was asking in either language. I gave her elfin body the larger part of my futon. She took off her clothes and lay with her tiny breasts spread flat over her ribcage so that only her nipple-ring stood up. In the lamplight from the street, I traced with my tongue the tattoo of thorns and roses encircling the top of her arm. I asked her about it, she had nothing to say. *It's old.* She brushed at my hair, sighing, her roses moving as the rest of her body arched in invitation. The only thing I really liked was her state of delectation. Let me enter her, flood her, swim in her, leave her unsatisfied, longing, dead. These possibilities weren't real. But for a moment a woman's body appeared to me an object. A clean reversal of all the times my body had been the one who says: *Take me, do what you want with me, fill me, open me, drown in me, kill me.* The next day, while chatting from the bathtub, I did not admit to Imogen what I had felt.

I knew, of course, there was a darker side to sex. The novels of Updike and Henry Miller and James Salter had sat on my parents' bookshelves alongside the bestsellers of the feminist canon from the 1970s and 80s. From those books I learned of bodily pleasure that contradicted the rules of communication and equality. Woman getting pinned down, thrown off-balance, cunts offered up like cut flowers, male desire so fierce there was no helping it, no excusing it, no explaining it, as shown in Miller's *The Rosy Crucifixion*:

'Please, please,' she begged, trying to squirm out of my embrace. 'You'll disgrace me.' I knew I had to let her go. I worked fast and furiously. 'I'll let you go,' I said, 'just one more kiss.' With that I backed her against the door and, without even bothering to lift her dress, I stabbed her again and again, shooting a heavy load all over her black silk front.

After my parents separated, my father kept a stash of *Playboy* magazines in a box under his bed – pictures of women whose hairless bodies gleamed like fish.

I asked myself what my father saw in those pictures. How he could like them, while telling me he didn't like nail polish and giving me Wollstonecraft's *A Vindication of the Rights of Woman* for my fourteenth birthday? The question became easier to answer as I read Updike and Miller. Historically, while the novel was a point of origin for individual subjectivity and political rebellion, novels could also make women into vulnerable bodies, objects to be looked at and raped. In eighteenth-century fiction, girls are spread out with alacrity, skirts pulled up, innocence stolen, dignity lost. Pamela would rather die than have any of these things done to her, but she writes hundreds of letters conjuring up the prospect of her own deflowering. Fanny Hill, another teenage letter-writer of the time, and star of the eighteenth century's most famous pornographic novel, surrenders her virginal body to an older woman by imagining herself naked from afar, *my shift being turned up to my neck, whilst I had no power or sense to oppose it; even my glowing blushes expressed more desire than modesty*. Both Fanny and Pamela are the invention of male writers, their first person narratives easy to critique. But they are also texts where men imagine themselves into female bodies, and where the eroticism of a woman's body is entangled with her elevation as a rational and political subject.

One of the novel's most delicate operations has been to appeal to a reader as a double agent of her own desire, to insist that sex exceeds and even contradicts the political and ideological categories of language she uses. Samuel

Richardson wrote for the clergy and the lusty seeker of entertainment, as well as with the knowledge that those people might be one and the same. Today Elena Ferrante writes for readers in adamant agreement about the fact that power and pleasure should be fairly distributed. And yet the sex she imagines is often difficult to align with a feminist point of view. Lenù, protagonist and first-person narrator of the *Neapolitan Quartet*, is aroused first by Donato, the worker poet. He kisses her at fifteen, then takes her virginity two years later on a beach outside the house while his family are sleeping. Lenù's onion-skinned orgasm that night flags the deep ambivalence she feels about *sex in itself, that unmediated demand for orgasm.* As a feminist writer, Lenù must reckon all her life with that *flow of pleasure* Donato has caused *against my very will.* That encounter on the beach is described in her first novel, the one for which Lenù becomes known as a feminist writer in Italy. We never find out how exactly Lenù's fictional story goes, but it's clear that Donato's approach, and her physical response to him, starts her account of female subjectivity and betrayal to life. In the televised version of the *Neapolitan Quartet* the beach scene becomes a rape, leaving Lenù physically unresponsive. But in the novel Lenù's pleasure is a grand and uplifting thing, a point at which Ferrante commits to that difficult suggestion that even politically liberated women might want sex, or at least fictions about sex, that undermine their better judgement.

As Shannon and I drove through Pennsylvania, feeling out all possible sites of difference and convergence between us, we talked about the Sex Wars of the late 1970s. My mother had been so clearly on one side of them, so committed to the fight for women's freedom from objectification and sexual exploitation. She and her lesbian friend next door had taken us to Take Back the Night marches, directed us to oppose things (movies, pictures, predators) that made women into bodies to be looked at, injured, oppressed, raped. In one rare moment of disciplinary intervention, my mother brought my brother out of his bedroom to talk about the politics behind those pictures in a magazine she found there. What women should want – my mother's side of the Sex Wars suggested – was to live in world of equality, not power-play; to be recognised rather than desired; to be shown in literature as clever and strong. But at one point in my thirties, as my mother was objecting in some way or another to bodies being seen as objects of desire, Hans said, *Do you think I love Tina in spite of her body; that I've never see her as an object?*

I was grateful for that point, for there being another side to the debate, a defence of pornography, sex-positive lifestyles, S&M, which Shannon could talk about with cheerful professionalism. After that trip, our first days together, she sent me an article in which two lesbians discuss the implications of occupying the positions of butch and femme in bed. What feminism is at risk of losing, one explains, is any sense of dimension: *when you say 'capture,' every fantasy you've ever heard of from Robin Hood to colonialism comes racing into your mind and all you really maybe wanted to do was have your girlfriend lay you down.* Their conversation redeems healthy sex as shot through with fantasy, with real and imagined differences. In that space of fiction, one can play at inequality without dividing up the real spoils of society. The article is not about novels, but insists more generally on there being places where sex has rules that are different from what is real.

I read that article on the day I was interviewed for a management job by a group of Danish men. If I was going to have an affair with someone in America, I couldn't work in England and live in Copenhagen. I wasn't going to travel less, but at least I needed to travel differently. I desperately needed a full-time job in Denmark. The men at the long boardroom table asked me to describe how I would promote more women at the university. I answered by unfurling my true political desire for gender equality. But if you'd asked me that day about fantasy, which is what Shannon was doing by sending that article, I wouldn't have named female empowerment. I wouldn't even have described wanting a more equal workplace, which I had good reason to want, and had argued for all my working life. I'd have described someone making me a Martini, someone I could push to the ground. I'd have described Shannon whispering *baby* in my ear while I cupped her breasts hard and did things to her without asking. I'd have described a novel in which I could be Donato without having to worry about Lenù's feelings at all.

I have little doubt about the erotic power of novels. But the fantasies they unleash are not necessarily the ones they seem to encourage. There's an unpredictability to the way fiction, like art and film, runs in and out of our bodies – a way books have of shaping our inner lives that censorship often fails to capture. Many of the reading rooms I have worked in as a researcher still have special desks reserved for the consultation of those books rated most pornographic. But what of the scenes we have conjured up under cover of the less well-protected page: the cherub's smile, the wounded nymph, the angle of the cowboy's hat as he leaves her behind in the dust? Rerouting our bodies, fiction makes room for scenarios other than the ones it actually represents. It does not choreograph its own reception.

In the end it was not Miller or Garner, or the lesbian fictions of Winterson, that turned me on as a teenager. It was not the novels that were good to women that I wanted to be in, but the ones that wrote me out of sex altogether. When I was seventeen and living back in London with my paternal grandmother, I worked in a supermarket close to Gay's the Word bookshop in Bloomsbury. There, in my lunch hour, I bought E. M. Forster's *Maurice* and read it on a bench in the park, explaining afterwards to my mother's incredulous friend that this was the very best of his novels. On the same bench I started Alan Hollinghurst's newly published *The Swimming Pool Library*, which tapped directly into some vein of my own lust. What I really found sexy was the disconsolate gay narrator, self-interested, insatiable in his appetite for casual sex. Living on supermarket sandwiches and reading in my attic bedroom in Barons Court, I coveted the life of the beautiful, independently wealthy Will, able to draw working-class boys into his Holland Park lair. I wished to be in his body, aroused by every Tube ride, seen by every man as an object of desire. How incontrovertible that kind of interest seemed; how desirable in itself, the possibility of wanting and being wanted as a body other than mine.

I liked above all the scene from *The Swimming Pool Library* in which Will forces his lover, who works in a hotel, to piss through his pants onto the kitchen floor, before having him kneel in the puddle. I couldn't have read it with a woman involved. I would have wondered too earnestly who was to clean the mess up. My taste for scenes in which one body overrules another did not extend far into the real realms of power. I did not want a woman doing mundane things for a man, did not want to read about lovemaking in which a woman's orgasm is hitched to her male lover's. As far as erotic reading went, I wanted scenes where sex had nothing to do with good communication, mutuality or collective responsibility. I secured these scenes' distinction from reality by accessing them in a form that shut me out. My identification with male bodies excited me more than anything I read involving women. It was only later, while reading Sedgwick, that I realised I was probably not alone: her desire, about which she is eloquent and often frank, is trained upon scenes of gay men or women disempowered.

The challenge for the historian of reading is not simply accounting for taste, but having real examples to hand of the illicit pleasures people have found in books. I am forcing myself to confess to the darkest sides of my reading pleasure because it would be an impropriety to try and guess at yours. Samuel Pepys read French pornography and admitted in his secret diary to buying the *idle, rogerish book L'escholle des filles*, stressing that he chose it in a cheap binding and planned to read it, if only as an education in the evils of the world. But while he was drunk that night he read it again and *burned it, that it might not be among my books to my shame*. More judicious than many today, with their mishandled Twitter accounts and incriminating browsing histories exposed to the harsh punishment of being read too literally, Pepys was an intelligent and conscientious member of Parliament, by all accounts an admirable administrator. His diaries were written in a code not properly deciphered until the nineteenth century; even so, the sexual details for which they are now well known were left out by editors who thought it best.

Simone de Beauvoir's letters were kept just as furtively from the public eye. If her niece hadn't betrayed her by publishing them, we'd never have known that the formative statements of twentieth-century feminism were written alongside descriptions of the simpering young women seduced in scenarios narrated for Sartre's pleasure. And we don't really know what kind of things Beauvoir read as models for those scenes, or if they came up straight out of her head. It's hard to describe this partial relation of our preferences in the realm of sex to the larger question of what we believe. It's hard to know who to prosecute, and who to blame for the discrepancies. In the majority of the books I have really loved, women are championed as agents of their own lives. In most classes I've taught we've critiqued women's objectification, problematised the optics of the male gaze. I've nurtured and read countless batches of essays in which students repeat back to me, sincerely, creatively, obediently, their misgivings about the sexism of fiction. I believe all this. I have no doubt that I have contributed in some small way, through the teaching and the writing I have done, to the rolling back of sexism and misogyny in my lifetime.

So it's not that I feel caught out exactly by the facts of my own fantasies, or that these help identify the electric force of what became possible in bed with Shannon, or that any of this points to where I stand as a scholar. My point is more about how loosely hinged these things all are to each other. The books I've read erotically are hidden only in plain sight. Many copies of *Fanny Hill*, *Venus in the Cloister* and *The Sofa: A Moral Tale* were burned in the 1700s, but now sit quite openly on institutional shelves. Henry Miller's *The Tropic of Cancer* is still sitting there gathering dust in my father's house, along with *The Joy of Sex*. I expect this pairing of 1970s texts – the one so ardent about female pleasure and communication, the other dripping as readily with misogyny as semen – recurs as their paperback editions wash up together in North London charity shops, getting shelved near the back by a slightly disapproving volunteer, close to the puzzles with missing pieces and the selections of cut-glass sugar bowls. *The Swimming Pool Library* is right there on the syllabus I'm teaching this term, which means I will finally have to give it the critical attention it deserves. I will talk to my students about the long history of the first-person narrator and the pornographic possibilities of this form; about the British Empire, the AIDS crisis, Thatcher's Britain; about whether Will is really meant to be a character at all. I will not talk about the ways that book lit up my imaginary and carefree cock.

Most novels have worked to align love and sex, but others have tackled quite seriously the desiring subject as a conflicted thing, raising that question of whether we ever find our greatest pleasures in scenes we rationally approve of. Hardy wrote in *Jude the Obscure* of sex that was so much better between Jude and Arabella than between Jude and Sue, who genuinely love and respect each other as they live for months without physical contact. The anomaly runs through Hardy's world like a small crack that cannot be fixed. It widens in Lawrence's *Sons and Lovers*, where Paul and Miriam, the truly communicative couple, fail in their physical connection. Paul spends years in the haystacks and flowerbeds with Miriam, admires from every angle her brown curls and full breasts, sees her naked as the perfect form. But though he diagnoses together with her the reasons for his reticence to kiss her, he cannot lose himself in her body. Of Clara, on the other hand, he is deeply critical, but he swoons in pleasure at the touch of her skin. The real intellectual match in *The Swimming Pool Library* is between Will and his closest friend, James. But Will, who gets aroused by almost anyone, is not aroused by James. Novelists reckon with this kind of rogue desire because they are manufacturers of fiction, proponents of the difference between fantasy and the real world.

The year I met Shannon was a bad one for the study of novels as a professional calling. Around the world, literature departments were failing to recruit majors; PhD students primed lovingly for succession weren't getting jobs; the humanities generally were out of favour with the governments in power. In England the tragic retrenchment of the twentieth-century project of state-funded humanities education was also in full swing. Fewer students than ever were studying literature, and those who did were likely to be asked what possible use such an education could be. A novel like *Jude*, with the question of working-class male fantasy so closely linked to a life of reading and freedom from convention, no longer pointed towards any clear set of improvements that any government was sponsoring. I felt all this as an intellectual and political loss. But more personally I felt bereft of the idea that desire might be worth studying hardest at a point where it is not firmly shackled to the real.

All around me that year I had heard and supported the language of sexual equality in relation to the exposure of sexual harassment. Some of my colleagues were being accused of having had sexual relationships with students, and even those who had not done this themselves felt under scrutiny. The conversations at academic gatherings had become strangely tense. A man I'd slept with as a student took me out for breakfast, wanting to know: *had he done me wrong?* Students spoke up against old writers and teachers in what felt sometimes like a rush of fresh air. But with the relief at hearing those old inequities exposed came my own memories of men who'd vacillated between being arrogant and needy and insistent. They did not seem like real culprits. I was pretty sure Imogen knew what she was up to, as she professed in the bath. But maybe the girl with the tattoo, a fellow occupant of a university world where I had the upper hand, had felt abused. I became queasy, reconsidering that night. But mostly I felt that bringing these misdemeanours to light would be easier if we weren't at the same time losing our grip on the study of fantasy. Literature is a realm where sexual offenders aren't always simply in the wrong; where it is possible to play at things you would not do in the flesh. *If you don't speak of fantasies*, I read that day of my interview, *they become a kind of amorphous thing that envelops you and hangs over your relationship and you get terrified of the silence.*

At the time I met Shannon, the university was also

becoming a place where any kind of actual sex was growing harder to talk about. There we were, people with jobs, with expensive shoes and glasses, listening in a mood of piety to talks about the stigmatised and the sexually harassed and newly trans-identified. But our old love lines – the experiments and mistakes, the flirtations between teachers and students, men and women – were growing fainter. Oh, Simone, you would not have survived, not even tenure. Pepys, you were complicated and conflicted, but so were we. I was surrounded at conferences by readers who were shrewd and funny, better at irony than most, but there was so much we could not say now, so many relationships in that very group that had grown cold. This did not mean it had all stopped, but it did make it harder to feel that language was a magic power. When Shannon was still a shoulder or two away from me, I sensed that I would give everything to lie down with her. Even in that season of correctitude, incorrect lust was a thing. Forty years after the Sex Wars, I was still asking what a woman wants, what it means to love one, what it might mean to risk other things that you believe in, just to find out.

It would be good to leave us idling here in each other's arms. If Connie Chatterley had been fucking the woman down the road instead of the gamekeeper, they might have kept lying there in the forest, enjoying different kinds of pleasures without having to get home for tea. If Anna's story in *The Golden Notebook* had been a bit less focused on men, perhaps those hallowed vaginal orgasms wouldn't have mattered so much, and Lessing could have worried less about ageing and realised how desirable older women could be. There's no reason to be fixated on the idea that you only get one shot, or that sex has to follow some narrative trajectory of its own, or that the timing has to be just so. Never the less, Shannon and I were rushing in our own way from one base to the next back then. Our little Pennsylvania road trip – those first days and nights in bed – was only our first tryst in that short season of jet-fuelled desire. During the next weeks we squeezed days and hours between other dates in our calendars, cancelled events we should have gone to, flew several times across the Atlantic, made new circuits of permission to do and say everything.

I got that management job in Copenhagen and went in April to London to pack up my English life, at least for a few years. Shannon met me there and we spent days lying in bed under a red quilt, the sun moving through all its positions while we talked. We read aloud from a novel then, the first part of Lisa Halliday's 2018 *Asymmetry*, which describes the sexual involvement of a young editorial assistant with a famous octogenarian novelist. In some ways this affair is even more politically incorrect than the one between Pamela and Mr B. Ezra has the money; Mary-Alice buys ice-cream for him and does clever things to his ageing body. But Mary-Alice is smart enough, and Ezra self-knowing enough, and Halliday a good enough writer, that *Asymmetry* slipped into public view in those early days of #MeToo. The pleasure of reading it with Shannon lay partly in this rubbing of history against the grain, feeling the close anatomy of a love affair in which those public lines of power do not hold quite true. But for me, it also had to do with listening to Shannon doing all the proper American voices, the baseball terms Ezra and Mary-Alice use being read in her Southern accent. The strumming of print, like a guitar.

The sex scenes between Mary-Alice and Ezra didn't relate very closely to what our bodies were up to. But when it comes to sex in fiction, the actual choreography often fades out of view. When Therese and Carol finally meet naked and in bed in *The Price of Salt*, green tendrils of desire shoot between them and a space opens up that is *beyond where thought could follow*. Therese's body becomes an arrow in that scene, crossing a wide canyon with ease and grace, leaving her clinging to Carol at the end of a long journey. *And she did not have to ask if this was right, no one had to tell her, because this could not have been more right or more perfect.* In the days that follow, the two of them take meandering drives in the mountains, along country roads to motels where they land again in bed together in the evening, knowing their bodies will find each other. Highsmith seems to be testing what it would mean to make pleasure a point of moral orientation, not a site of representation.

Then there's that scene in *Another Country* where Eric and Vivaldo wake together after a long night of drinking and talking. Each of them is utterly entangled in another relationship: Eric with Yves, and Vivaldo with Ida. But for that day they are bewilderingly and hungrily lost in each other's bodies. As Vivaldo lies with his hand around Eric's penis, he recalls at first every fantasy of violence and penetration he has had, brings every phantom woman he's known into the scene. But in the end he just gives himself over to what is happening: *it was like making love in the midst of mirrors, or it was like death by drowning. But it was also like music, the highest, sweetest, loneliest reeds, and it was like the rain.* This is a scene that cannot be fully told, yet in the middle of it Vivaldo asks himself a question for which the sex itself seems already to have supplied the answer: *what virtue were they seeking, now, to share?*

It's tempting to read these scenes as ones where Baldwin and Highsmith begin to write about gay or lesbian bodies, and the kinds of futures that can be imagined for those couples. At last Carol and Therese know that they want each other. At last Eric can be himself without shame. But they are also scenes where the pleasure of all scripts falls away, and position-taking becomes possible without the promise that anything has to hold from one frame to the next. I did not, in that brief, delirious patch of early spring with Shannon, say or write much about what was actually happening in bed. But I felt fuller of the joy of sex than I ever had before, and drunk from one moment to the next on the pleasure of her existence. Back in Copenhagen, Hans and I agreed that I would find my own flat and I began to imagine the joy of pulling Shannon and her suitcase into it.

Chapter Six

ONE-WAY LOVE

I felt ashamed that spring to have spent my life studying a literary form that contends best with adultery as something that sends characters hurtling towards disaster. Yes, I had defended literature's loose relation to reality, advocated the way fictional worlds need be true only to themselves. But my real life – the one I didn't talk about with students – had begun to feel so charmed in contrast to all the lives I read about, in which the plot points either towards marriage or towards death. That was true up until the night when Shannon nearly died.

We were lying together on what was meant to be our last night in London when she described her headache. As she talked, telling me she needed to sleep, her voice began to slur. I had to drag myself out of the nest of pleasure and remember to foresee disaster. I rang an NHS number and they sent an ambulance, whose medics came crashing into our room and took control of the scene. They packed Shannon in her linen nightshirt onto a stretcher, rushed us through the red lights of King's Cross. In the ambulance I held Shannon's bare feet as they grew cold and she slipped into unconsciousness. Many hours later she was delivered back to the intensive-care ward where I had waited, her voice gone and her body wired up on every side.

Deep in the night, I called her American friends and family and explained that Shannon had had a stroke so serious that she might die. Delivering that information made it clear how much had not been said about what we were doing. Who was I, to be translating this possibility of her death to people who knew her better? Why was she even in London? *I am her partner*, I told the doctors, willing this relationship into reality, urging them to let me camp in the waiting room, hoping that I was legitimate enough to be there. I called Hans in Copenhagen, leaving him to explain to other people what was happening. With many kinds of agency miraculously suspended, my new role was to listen to the facts that the doctors, and the machines that forced the mechanical breaths between Shannon's lips, might tell. Eventually those voices said she would live.

I shuttled all that April between Bloomsbury, where Shannon lay in hospital, and my new job in Copenhagen, which I squeezed into a few days a week. I sat dazed in meetings that I could hardly understand, and took planes and trains before dawn, forgetting sometimes where I was. I spoke with Rohan and Marie about things that were small and concrete, cooked them meals and gave them books bought at the airport. Then I went to the ward and joined the group who had gathered around Shannon – riveted to the first opening of her eyes, the removal of the tubes, the sound of her voice coming back, hushed but sweet. I arrived some mornings at the door of the ward before the nightshift was over, claiming that first moment alone with her. Sweet and lazy-eyed, she met me with hands bruised by the needles, her lips tasting like iodine. There is a lot to say about those weeks, her return to life, the first day we took her wheelchair outside into the pale sun. Shannon's brother sat through it all, keeping faithful watch on a diet of cheese and toast from the nearby hotel. People from all the parts of her life collided in grief, an army of warriors fighting for her, in and out of her wild dreams.

What Shannon missed was London in the clutches of that precocious summer: leaves unfolding fast, crocuses lolling back after their early bloom onto the earth. Leaving her ward, I'd walk along the paths of Russell Square as the traffic roared and watch tourists drinking expensive coffees at a pace. The Italian ice-cream café advertised for extra staff because of the precipitous warmth. My friends in town for anti-Brexit events met me at the tables in the park, ordering *gelato* or sparkling water and wondering at my tale. Appropriately, Westminster was where real and fictional lands met. Shannon lying there half conscious while Clarissa Dalloway ran around, preparing for her party, buying flowers, her mind sweeping around in big arcs through time and space, focused on the evening ahead. *Like the pulse of a perfect heart*, her old love thinks in June, *life struck straight through the streets*. Shannon living again, while Will from *The Swimming Pool Library* meets his lovers in what used to be the Russell Square Hotel.

When Shannon took her first steps, many people watched as if eye-beams might hold her up. The staff brought her through the swing doors to practise on the hospital's Victorian staircase. Two steps, rest, up three, rest. While the physical therapists monopolised her body, the rest of us noted with a pride that soon became absurd the progress Shannon made, the animals of bright-green playdough she produced in physical therapy, the depths of her humour coming back. *What is your partner's name?* the doctor asked her when checking her pulse a week after the stroke, not gauging the full import of her replying with a slow tongue, *Is this a trick question?* April was when I was forced to answer that question for myself – to make of falling in love a fully-fledged account of how to live a life, and how to bring one to a close. *I am going to be with her,* I told Hans one night in Copenhagen.

This might be an ending. But that whole mix of agency at an ebb, and crisis in the air, feels now like it was only a rehearsal for the possibility of living in a world authored by some mysterious force. Since Shannon's stroke, most things in the larger world have become too unruly and diffuse to qualify as plot. During the autumn of 2019 Shannon grew strong and mobile again. But history became raw incomprehensibility – our own little drama of adultery and passion humbled in the mix. A year after Shannon survived, we sat in Copenhagen studying reports of the global pandemic as if they were jigsaw pieces, lacking any board to lay them on. Plans crumpled all around us; things that once seemed non-negotiable became dispensable. When the bubonic plague came to London in 1665, people walked around holding smelling salts under their noses without considering the fleas travelling with the mice under every door, spreading the disease between humans. Their disjointed relationship to a big picture that they could not see, their fierce desire to protect the ones they loved, had become so obvious to me.

The year of 2020: a year of great fires, infection, violence, political upheaval; of Shannon being with me much longer than we could have planned; of solid joy in the midst of everything else. There was new evidence everywhere of our unwise species, of our biological vulnerability, of huge change being possible. We focused on small acts of finding ourselves still alive – climbing the steps, making love. Shannon's stroke and recovery felt somehow like a foretaste of the pandemic and its silver lining. The first backdrop of the stroke was the smog of London lit up with an encroaching summer, life brought to a personal stop by Shannon's blood not flowing. The next spring of her recovery, there was a much broader backdrop of urban hush. We lived in a small flat down the road from the one I'd once shared with Hans, taking slow laps of our common cobbled precinct each afternoon. The skies were hoovered clean of planes, and the water in the canal settled into blueish-green, a pure surface looking back. Swans built trashy nests where tourists' paddleboats used to go. Pink and orange town houses glowed, resplendent from people having so much extra time. Their owners hung from newly painted window frames in the middle of the day. As I had once imagined, Hans came for dinner, bought rye bread, and together we tried to entertain Rohan and console Marie for the lives they had lost. We became a small bubble of people thrown together, in and out of love and luck. I found myself writing this book about love and the novel, but narrative itself failed me in yet new ways.

Waterstones reported a significant rise in book sales in 2020, but I did not read much more than usual that year. Partly it was the magnetic pull of the newspapers, lit up under the bedcovers at night on a phone. In the 1700s booksellers complained that when world events got interesting, news was the only thing people would buy. I split the difference by reading a lot that was written in the 1970s, that decade of my own childhood: for instance, Elizabeth Hardwick and Robert Lowell's painful post-separation letters, reassembled with editorial care as magical as authorship. Lowell is living now with Caroline, his new wife, with whom he has a new child. Hardwick is mostly in their old apartment in New York, which she shares with Harriet and a housekeeper. I, the adulterer, read these letters aloud in my rented apartment to my new lover, who can no longer read the way she did before the stroke, no longer do the voices. I identify perversely with Hardwick, the one who is left organising things, worrying over the damp in the house in Maine.

The small drama of that long-ago divorce unfolds against the anti-Vietnam protests, students shot by the police, Nixon's presidency, feminists lobbying in Washington. The letters cover the day Shannon was born in 1970, and the day I was born a year later. Hardwick is invested in that riotous history, but not in the way my parents were, with their bodies and their class positions on the line. As a writer in her forties, she stays off to the side, out of the fray. Harriet may want to cycle around Europe, but she should first do well at private school. It's difficult to say if Hardwick's perspective counts as political. Scholars of Jane Austen have always had a hard time saying how political her commitments were. Austen wrote against a world shaped by the Napoleonic Wars and the threat of revolution in England, but she was so obviously committed primarily to fiction as her form. There is a branch of scholarship that says she didn't notice, or wasn't interested in, democracy or women's rights or abolition, so conservative on this count compared to Wollstonecraft and Paine. Yet every word Austen wrote was affected by the paper shortage that the wars brought, and by the traffic in communication that defined the period. There's barely a scene in *Pride and Prejudice* where the soldiers aren't stationed somewhere nearby.

Moments of historical chaos have been hard in their own right for novelists to record. When one is inside them, it's difficult to see how any kind of single perspective could be won. *War and Peace* grapples with the impossibility of reconciling the soldier's view of the battle with the official account of war. Scale and credibility and responsibility all present challenges to the narrator and his perspective. *The Magic Mountain*, that story of Castorp and his cousin, of Clawdia loved in the Alps, is set against the background of the First World War and predicts the comforts of the German merchant class and the intellectuals being about to end. Mann started *The Magic Mountain* in 1912, writing on during that whole catastrophic decade without actually moving his attention to the battlefields, not until the last chapters when Castorp ends up there, and all of the sanatorium's slow, pampered lives are relativised by that reality of mass death.

Mrs Dalloway hosts her summer party in 1923. Not much of her reported thinking relates directly to the war that has just ended, and yet everything Clarissa thinks is connected in some way to it having happened. The plane making letters in the sky for the purposes of advertising is visible as not an instrument of violence; and the suicide announced as a piece of news at the book's close registers as one of the war's casualties. Parts of *The Swimming Pool Library* are set in the hotel next to the hospital where Shannon lay. Hollinghurst wrote that novel as the AIDS crisis threatened Europe. In his lifetime and mine, thirty-two million people have died worldwide of that epidemic. Will's exuberance about the possibilities of sex up in Phil's staff bedroom is inextricable from that.

Thirty-two million is too many to write a novel about; the forty million who died in the First World War are better captured indirectly through one death than as an honest tally. It's going to be hard to make those millions of Covid-19 deaths into a story. When Daniel Defoe published in 1719 what is arguably the world's first real novel, *Robinson Crusoe*, he had been puzzling for a while over how to bring a mass event to light through its composite parts. In 1704 he assembled eye-witness accounts of Britain's biggest-known storm, making local instances evident as one larger story of devastation. Twenty years later he wrote *A Journal of the Plague Year*, a fictional account of the Great Plague of London told through the eyes of a saddler who stays in the city watching people leave, reporting the suffering of those around him and counting the casualties. Over the spring and summer of 1665 he notes the locked-up houses, the bans on movement, the increasing poverty, the slim odds of his own survival.

A Journal of the Plague Year's fictional narrator is an observer of facts. There's no particular industry or intelligence behind his staying alive. He relates second-hand tales of individuals who do, and do not, make it. A mother sees the telltale spots on the skin of the baby at her breast, and it dawns on her from one minute to the next that both she and the child will die. A drunk man leaps alive from the mass grave where he has accidentally been buried, after falling asleep in the cart that collects the bodies. A well-dressed traveller from out of town expires at the inn before the maid can serve him his warm ale. The narrator presents the facts; he has survived. But there is no evidence that anyone like him existed – someone who would care enough about the world to hold all the parts in view, rather than being absorbed into it.

The thing Defoe invents is the individual as saviour and narrator of his own life. *Robinson Crusoe* is one fictional man's take on history: colonialism, the slave trade, a storm. The events in the background are big historical travesties. But the story through which they are recalled focuses on Crusoe's personal industry. He has escaped and has tamed nature. As he weaves baskets, makes clay pots, salvages things from shipwrecks and turns grapes to raisins, his property accumulates. Even his money, invested in slave plantations while he's on the island, increases. History yields to the force of individual ambition and survival. While *Robinson Crusoe* declares that everything is in God's hands, it is effort and structural inequality that drive this new kind of narrative.

There will no doubt be many novels set in 2020, about characters whose worlds were stopped by death, or who fell in love at the moment when everything went quiet, or worked to save people becoming sick or hungry around them. New reports are already being written about people negotiating those variously quiet and angry streets and hospital wards. But it will be hard to capture with a naked eye the larger whole of which these individual stories are insignificant parts. Since Shannon's stroke I have felt that history on its largest scale, and the body on its smallest, are equally hard to account for. I have felt the dialling-down of my own power over questions of life, or getting to live at all. Whether it's because the ambulance is too slow, or because the ship breaks too violently against the rocks of the island, or because the mass graves outside the city walls fill up too quickly, this feeling of radically reduced agency is hard to square with fiction. Novelists have had to contend with contingency as they have written anthems for a secular world, for characters who survive and make a profit, for lovers who get to choose and to act.

I do not want to renege on that sense that novels are about agency. They enjoin us to think for ourselves, to change our minds: this has been in their DNA from the beginning. But I've set aside this chapter to reckon with that other thing – the way that reading them makes us witnesses of events and characters in stories that we don't control, cases where our readerly or writerly care makes no difference. Novels are distinct from the real world in its contingency and its scale. And yet through our investment in the people they represent, we learn what it means to care intensely about aspects of reality that we cannot change. Fictional characters do not need us – the readers who love them. We live, as the critic Andrew Miller puts it, in a state of *peculiarly askew intimacy with them*. Their bodies are paper and ink. Much that I feel about the world seems tried and tested at this range, provoked by relations that are exclusive of my participation, by narrative forces as indifferent to me as the forms of liquid inevitability in evidence in both pandemic and stroke.

Sometimes, when teaching classes on Jane Austen, I try to describe this impotency. I come as the bearer of bad news, bringing to the table that deflating reminder: Elizabeth Bennet is not your friend. Austen's characters cannot write or talk to you. They cannot learn from you. You cannot claim them as feminist comrades, when they were invented long before the cause as we know it. Whatever they teach about love can apply only to you, to your actual people, who are likely to behave disappointingly in comparison to those buoyed up by fiction. Yet this state of powerlessness is not a hopeless thing. Sometimes great knowledge incubates under these conditions of ineffectiveness. In Miller's terms, reading reveals our *burden of perfection*, the strange load we lift as we open a novel, prepared to feel things for characters we cannot save. By looking into that one-way mirror of example, we sign up for belonging to a world that is finished, but relevant, for all that, to our own becoming.

When Shannon was close to death that first week after the stroke, I watched her lying there and wondered what it would mean if she could never write back. The affair we were having was in its infancy. I hadn't begun to be with her as I wanted to. Perhaps, I concluded in the dark hours when I pined for her to come back, it would not matter if her hands no longer moved, her legs stayed still, her eyes stopped properly meeting mine. I would keep on loving her in any physical state as long as she could signal somehow that she was there. But after a few days of her being unconscious, I felt laden with letters I could not reasonably send. Only talking with her again would unburden me of that feeling.

Without dialogue, my new understanding, even of death, felt dumb and fruitless. Falling in love, writes Eve Kosofsky Sedgwick, involves believing that *another person represents your only access to some ... radiantly heightened mode of perception*. To lose that *thread of intimacy* is to know that you must *subsist forever in some desert-like state of ontological impoverishment*.

Many who survive strokes like Shannon's enter a state of irreversible physical lockdown. Those who love them must cross a gulf of unresponsiveness as absolute as the one dividing the reader from the character on the screen or page. Only by way of memory and fierce acts of imagination can lovers and children and friends incapacitated by disability or death conjure up a dialogue that will never again exist – one that may or may not be happening in the mind of the person intubated or unconscious, unable to speak. So many people have imagined their way across that distance during the pandemic, barred from wards and bedsides, unable to say anything in person to the one that all their thoughts come addressed to. In this sense, I was lucky in getting to wait for the words, for the first tiny gleams of Shannon's old self being there at arm's reach.

Yet I have loved before under conditions where there was no obvious pathway of return. Not just as a reader, a fan of certain people observed from the sidelines, a mute participant of history, but in those first weeks of being mother to Marie, a baby born weeks too early. She slept and drank as if she were still in the world of the womb, hardly responsive to touch. In the middle of the night Hans would wake her and force my milk between lips that opened, closed and sucked

on a tiny plastic teat, her mouth a strange single-celled creature, taking in nourishment without thought. My thoughts
looped endlessly back to the basket where she slept. Was
that love? In *Anna Karenina*, Levin, who hopes to be over-
whelmed with feeling for his newborn son, is disappointed.
*I expected more. I expected that a new, pleasant, feeling would
blossom in me like a surprise. And suddenly, instead of that,
there was squeamishness, pity.* As Marie hung like a mario-
nette from Hans's outstretched hand, my heart rioted with
feeling. But when I went that month of her birth to see a
film about a disturbed nurse who loves a patient in a coma,
tending and talking to her as if she were awake, I was horri-
fied by the parallels. Loving a baby so tiny was delusional,
an investment in a connection that might one day happen,
rather than any kind of reciprocal bond.

A year or so later, a friend asked me to stay the evening
with her six-month-old son. She had never left the baby
before. The friend warned me that he wouldn't go to sleep
for me: he would lie awake and cry. She – the friend – would
never be able to go out again. In fact the baby cried. In
despair, I offered my dry breast. The baby sucked and slept,
oblivious to the change of guard – a traitor to his parent's
fidelity. Would any breast have done? It's only quite recently
in historical terms that we would have described this physical entanglement as love. Even as people were reading novels
in which lovers became individuals, infants were routinely
disqualified in fiction as proper sites of deep care. Moll Flanders, protagonist and narrator of Defoe's second novel, has
so many children that she finds them hard to track, and most
of them drop out of the story along the way.

But if biological children only became such strong con-
tenders for love recently, there was, in the early days of the
novel, great understanding of what sympathy for a child or
a patient or a prisoner viewed from a distance might be. The
fact that the plight of another could make bystanders feel
so much was important evidence of our humanity. Through
imagination, the philosopher Adam Smith wrote, we enter
into such a powerful state of identification with the prisoner
on the rack that his pain becomes our own. Levin's first real
wave of feeling for his son comes as he sees a tree fall in a
storm, picturing it landing on the pram. It is not a scene of
action: Levin knows that if the tree has crushed the baby, it's
already happened. But it is a scene of love, one in which the
distance separating Levin from his family, and his sense of
being unable to help, prompts the pitch of protective feeling
that he had expected to arrive at earlier. Certain kinds of
critical distance can work as a nutrient to feeling. There is
something about such a remove that is conducive to what the
critic Adela Pinch describes as love-thinking: an engagement
of absolute tenderness with someone who is not immediately
present or receptive to care.

Just before Shannon's stroke I'd been teaching André Alexis's
Fifteen Dogs, a slow-burning success of 2015. The novel begins
with the kind of unrealistic premise I usually have no taste
for. Two gods go into a bar and have a dispute about the sad
state of human beings. As a result, they end up giving a group
of dogs an enhanced capacity to speak in complex terms
of reason and emotion: let's see, the bet goes, if *this* makes
them happy. The dogs quickly develop a language with all the

nuances, idioms and artistic potential of humans. They com-
pose beautiful sentences and fall in love. Almost instantly
the simplicity of their canine life is ruined. As interactions
become more complex, the community grows fraught, hier-
archical and murderous. Language only leads, it seems, to
misery. But two of the dogs use their new linguistic skill pro-
ductively. Prince, a noble mutt, becomes a poet, preserving
his dialect, focusing on linguistic perfection. And Majnoun,
the black poodle, learns the language of Nina – the human
he lives with. These approaches pull in two very different
directions, but both make communication a prize worth
fighting for: for Prince, language is something that leaves the
poet lonely but expressive in his art, while for Majnoun, language is what makes it possible to leap across the huge divide
between otherwise-alien minds.

When I was preparing to teach *Fifteen Dogs* I thought
the novel would be too contrived for its argument in favour
of language to work with the students. I read the book a
second time on the train to campus. Shannon was arriving
in London from New York the next day. I was immune to
small worries, lost in anticipation, my mind filled with things
I needed to say to her. Obviously I was on Majnoun's side in
believing that love was communication. But in the classroom
I snapped to attention. The students discussed *Fifteen Dogs*
more keenly than they had any novel we had read that term.
They sat on the edge of their seats, explaining how much they
liked it, and how strongly they related to the moral dilemmas
that come with consciousness. Perhaps they had opened it
for the animal story, or the whiff of *Percy Jackson*, but clearly
the possibilities that Alexis lays out were real for them. As a

motley bunch of English majors – many of them the first in their families to be studying at all – they felt Prince's predicament. Language can be a source of happiness and love, but it can also alienate you from your immediate family. It can catapult you into new relations, things more complex than any novel or poem suggests, but it then deprives you of one-way love. All of it is so much harder than the kind of unconditional feeling that a child or an animal or a character elicits.

After that class, I saw Alexis as interested in something that novelists have worried about from the beginning, which is how a world made of language – one with which the reader can never really interact – might fail or measure up to the challenges of real relations between different people. Historically, as novel worlds grew more and more realistic, readers had to be reminded that the perfect loves they showcased were inadequate templates for their own connectedness to the world. *Don Quixote, The Female Quixote, Northanger Abbey, Adeline Mowbray*: these are all early fictions about characters weaned off their love for language in order to be better aligned with the people around them. In *The Female Quixote*, Arabella learns crushingly that real love does not come with the high drama and adventure for women that drives French Romance. In *Northanger Abbey*, Catherine must stop imagining a world of Gothic novels, in order to settle down to marriage. Almost every one of Jane Austen's characters adjusts what she has learned of love from novels, relinquishing her first love, those bookish impressions. A chastened Emma accepts that relations in her small village cannot be brokered or read like stories; that her feelings for Knightley, too familiar to be recognised at first by her romantic self, are in fact of the deepest kind. Realism evolves by breaking the spell of words.

This sense that romance must be reconciled with reality is also there in *Anna Karenina*. By the end of the novel Anna and Vronsky's story has run its tragic course. Levin, newly married to Kitty and living on his country estate, has spent his summer reading philosophy, looking for an answer to the question of whether a God exists. He reaches his conclusion that day of the rainstorm, when he imagines the tree falling on Kitty and the baby. Larger meaning, he realises, is not found in books, but in the conduct of simple activities. He may never know God, but he knows how to handle his bees, work the threshing machine, talk with Kitty in the evening. Levin concludes that if transcendence is possible, it can be experienced only through action. And he sees that even this epiphany is answerable to its own logic. Drunk with insight, he tries to treat his coachman with respect. He watches his infant son, safe and fussed over; listens to Kitty's worries about the household; struggles in these domestic settings to hold on to the elated feelings he's experienced that day. *Anna Karenina* ends with the insistence that an abstract love for humanity must be reconciled with the love of living people. Neither transcendent understanding nor conversational exchange is enough; neither great distance nor absolute proximity will do; neither everyday dialogue nor the grand thinking that leaves one alone. It is Levin's triumph, and Tolstoy's, and Austen's, and Alexis's, to keep this compromise in mind even as they write. Even the perfect novel, the perfect one-way expression of love, must measure up to dialogue.

*

Once Shannon was properly conscious again, her appetite for interaction was fierce. Unable to talk clearly, she lay in her bed, making friends with the nurses and doctors. Besotted with her aliveness, I was not surprised that the people looking after her could intuit how funny and deserving of empathy she was. She asked us to play pop songs and advertising jingles from the 1970s. She recalled film scores, things that repeated, her childhood in couplets, memories of her siblings playing a game or eating Hamburger Helper. At some point she moved on to poems and we became her DJs, dialling up from the depths of the internet sonnets and elegies, reading them aloud. *Let's have Elizabeth Bishop*, she said as we lay together on the narrow bed, pill bottles and liquid nutrient piled up on the table in a sunbeam. I found 'Crusoe in England' on my phone, the poem she wanted for its image of islands upon islands birthing from one's head.

Without knowing them beforehand, I read to her those lines of damp, lonely green and violet-blue. They are told in the voice of a disillusioned Crusoe, restored to London but wistfully recounting his years among tropical clouds and giant turtles, goats and gulls. Defoe's Crusoe – the archetypical Protestant man – is always busy in isolation, plotting, writing in his diary, farming, preparing for the next season, discovering God. In Bishop's poem he recalls himself being at ease, his legs swinging from the crater of a volcano, painting a baby goat red, just to get something new into the mix. More than action, survival entails such aesthetic attention. On the island there was *one of everything*: one tool, one snail, one sun. Back in the real world Crusoe regrets this loss of singularity.

I wondered if Shannon was missing the way it felt to live adrift in an ocean of morphine, to feel the words washing back into her brain; to track, wondrous and original, the sterilised objects wobbling into her blighted vision – faces from New York and Philadelphia and Kentucky turning up out of place. Catheters and kidney-shaped dishes, cornflakes for breakfast. Had they kept her company? Was she less lonely now or keen to return to the dreams she'd had of all of us? Bishop's poems are so finely detailed. They give the things that come her way the visibility they have on Crusoe's island. One fish's eyes and a magazine page from a certain day loom large and ripely meaningful. But in real life, in an early letter to Lowell, Bishop describes herself as profoundly alone. She hardly wrote about her great love, the Brazilian architect Lota de Macedo Soares, or her many losses.

Bishop exchanged letters with Lowell throughout his lifetime. Some of them are ones I've read this year. It seems a funny friendship, given how different they were, and how strongly Bishop disapproved of the poetry he wrote after his leaving Hardwick. In 1972, the year Bishop published 'Crusoe in England', Lowell was already living in Kent with Caroline. In his study, an elongated room with a view of sheep in a field, he was constantly losing things (brochures for art classes Harriet might take, divorce papers) and missing sentimental ones (pictures of Hardwick, books from their now decommissioned house in Maine). There in the study he wrote the intensely personal 'Dolphin' poems for which even his friends reproached him. His 1973 collection takes, as Bishop pointed out, excruciating liberties with reality, cribbing Lizzie's letters and using them in his autobiographical pastiche, putting what had been a dialogue through the one-person mill of lyric narration. His splicing of real words into his poetry suggests that he failed to see the difference between birthing islands out of one's head and living ethically in the land of two-way conversation.

Bishop might have had Lowell in mind when she was putting the final touches to 'Crusoe in England'. Some of Crusoe's haplessness – his feeling of not being actually responsible for his own romantic mess – suggests this:

'Was there a moment when I actually chose this? I don't remember, but there could have been.'

Crusoe's failure to reconcile worlds is reminiscent of Lowell, bent on making what Bishop sees as the deepest kind of category mistake. To write of someone is not to love them. To have loved them is not to win the right to write about them. Especially when they can't write back. When Hardwick, in an essay otherwise admired, described Elizabeth Bishop's lover, Lota, as a Brazilian discontent unhappy with household arrangements in Maine, Bishop stepped in to correct her. If this is Lota you have in mind, she says in friendly but firm tones to Hardwick, Lota would not have said it like that, or lisped while doing so. Writing to Lowell in a similar mood, Bishop quotes Thomas Hardy: *What should certainly be protested against, in cases where there is no authorization, is the mixing of fact and fiction in unknown proportions. Infinite mischief would lie in that.* If you must write about it all, at least get it right.

Defoe put his Crusoe on a fictional island. There was a

reported case of a real survivor in such a setting in the 1700s. But Defoe invented this one, ringing his character around with seas of paper harder to cross than coral reefs. Crusoe could not get off the page because to do so would have been the miscegenation of two universes, fiction and reality. This did not stop many early readers believing the novel to be a true account of something; or hoping, as in the case of *Pamela* or *Pride and Prejudice*, that they might sleep with or befriend these characters themselves. But the very fact of Pamela and Crusoe being fictional protects them from the harm and consolation that love brings. These are different realms of love, as Bishop insists: one in which the poet can say all she will, tend to a word-garden as she likes, without fear of company or misappropriation – and another in which she must face up to the real conundrums of life.

Hardwick accepted Bishop's rebuke about Lota graciously. *Sleepless Nights* accounts carefully, like Bishop's poems, for things she has seen: a yellow ball dropped from a window by a child, a basket of laundry carefully arranged by someone good at ironing. Lowell is not there, nor Harriet, nor Lota. Some Southerners and Europeans from the past appear; and the barn in Maine, rebuilt once Lowell finally finds in his office those legal papers confirming that it belongs to Hardwick. But the working people in the novel are as distant as if they lived in a foreign land. Imagine, she writes, what it would be like to live with a man like the ones who come to work on the barn. *I find myself falling into a flirtatiousness, a sort of love for their look, their sun burned faces, their fine oiled workshoes, their way at the wheel of a truck, their jokes about the bill, their ways with other men.* To live with a carpenter, she guesses, would be to watch him coming out of the shower and sitting down to dinner at six before lovemaking. It would also be not to travel, not to have him fix things at home, not to exist as a character at all. One-way love can be like this, a display of words unlikely to be read by those involved. The dead are helpful here, and the illiterate, and the unconscious, the stranger on the rack – all inspiring us to feel deeply and observe closely the potential for dialogues we are not in. For obvious reasons, I do not want to dismiss this kind of love-thinking entirely.

One reason that the narratives we read and write about are unlike real events has to do with the physics of time. Things that get written down must have happened in order for us to be reading about them. Although Richardson experimented in *Pamela* with having her write right up until that moment when she gets kissed or overpowered, it's hard to keep going in the present tense. When the tree falls in the last chapter of *Anna Karenina*, Levin reprimands himself for imagining that he could do anything: if the baby is to be crushed by it, he will be. That's how fiction works. There's no interventionist god powerful enough to change the lives led in a published novel. A narratologist would say this was a truism – novels always being over even as they are still happening. You are right in the middle of the story, but you cannot tell Elizabeth to hurry up and get together with Darcy. Or shout at Connie Chatterley that he's not worth it. Or tell Anna not to jump in front of that train. All you can do is read about those lives over and over again, with full knowledge of what is to come. Those characters are bound to make mistakes, and we are bound to delight in subtle ways in them being unavertable. Real love should not be like this.

There's a way in which fiction always having already run its course makes it possible to look ahead, around the corner, into its future. Prolepsis – the possibility of seeing the present from that point of view – happens in novels in ways it does not in real life. *When I was in my forties*, states Helen Garner in an essay written many years after *Monkey Grip*, *I went on holiday to Vanuatu with a kind and very musical man to whom I would not much longer be married, though I didn't know it yet.* This is the spirit in which Austen can say with assurance that Catherine Morland was born to be a heroine, even when she seems in *Northanger Abbey*'s opening pages to be nothing of the sort; or can joke that we know a happy ending is coming because we see the telltale compression of the pages in our hand. A fictional character lives by this logic in the thrall of a narrator who knows what lies ahead.

Reality has no such future exterior. I can think back now to Shannon and me looking at the ducks in the park, talking about ornithology and planning a course that we wanted to teach, just hours before she had her stroke. I can look at us all flying around the world. I can see Marie on her trip to China in January of 2020. But only in a novel could I have written: *the tall schoolgirl with the long blond hair would not travel again for almost two years.* I view us all back then with the kind of tenderness that hindsight brings: that last dinner with friends before the first lockdown; the last summer Hans and I spent together with the kids in Sweden before I met Shannon. But I can't know what is coming next. The strokes and plagues in real life are as unavoidable as those in novels, though the two kinds of contingency are completely different.

Once Shannon was out of rehab in June, we went on a trip to Virginia. We played word games and found out that Shannon was still the best. On a beach we lay so quietly that spindly crabs came out, poked around and scuttled away again as clouds drifted high over us. We took a novel from a bag filled with oranges and bagels we'd pilfered from the Holiday Inn breakfast bar and finished *Asymmetry* lying there on the sand, months after we'd begun reading it aloud. At the point we were reading it again, Halliday's vindication of intergenerational love seemed less important than the case she makes for the writer's capacity for great empathy. Ezra says you must write about what you know. But Mary-Alice says that fiction is also an occasion to sympathise with someone other than yourself, someone whose plight you can understand even if you are not in it, or able to change it. She proves this by becoming the assumed author of the second part of *Asymmetry*, which describes the experience of a man caught up in an immigration nightmare of the kind Mary-Alice is unlikely ever to have had herself.

By the time I was reading the second half of that novel, its content was drowned out by the significance of it being possible to pick up and go on with any kind of story. Shannon was looking now at the world in a way that was hard for me to imagine. She wasn't taking her old turns at reading to me, could no longer drive, needed long naps each day. As I read *Asymmetry* aloud, she was lying with the sun on her face, squinting up at me when I came to a good bit of the story. Her eyes had been left half operational by the stroke. A tiny bit of tissue gone astray in the operation that saved her had made it impossible for her to read, even though she could see the crabs scuttling around, the shoreline milky at our feet, the freckles coming out on her skin. She could remember the beginning of the novel better than those months she'd been in hospital. We were happy, but Hans and Rohan and Marie and the many people who loved Shannon had suffered deeply since the stroke, which had forced us so dramatically together. All that pain, all that distance, all that love in the world.

Shannon has spent most of the global pandemic with her little earbuds in, consuming fiction and news. Led by what was available in audio form in the libraries, and by apps that provide good journalism read out loud, and by technology that spells her students' work out to her in a mechanical voice that startles me when I hear it by accident, she races through words from morning to night. I'm not sure why I ever worried about her not being able to read. When I ask if she wants lunch or a walk, she takes the earbuds out, shakes her head clear of sound, pulls back from whatever story she's in. Sometimes she tells me what she's been listening to as we walk or sit eating meals together. The election results. *Barnaby Rudge*. Environmental racism in Pennsylvania. The fish dying in Ghana. *War and Peace*. It was Shannon who told me, for instance, about the soldier who knows so little of what is going on in the battles he's fighting that he relies on people who were not actually there to tell him about the history he's been a part of. When it's me reading to Shannon, I'm a minor player in a chorus of professional readers who have been occupied for as long as there have been books turning ink into air.

Sometimes that kind of alchemy has been pedagogical and unwelcome. The history of audiobooks has meant that unorthodox and blind readers have had to contend with having less to choose from than sighted ones. *War and Peace* is actually on pause, because Shannon didn't get through all fifty hours of it before it was due back to the library. The whole idea of language changes when you imagine novels poured unevenly into the ear by an unfriendly voice, or when you can't read at all. I have a new sense that bodies might have some say in the matter of whether words work – whether they get through. It's not just words all the way down. But it can be movingly companionate, this reading together: there's something of that first era of the novel in it, whole families gathered around the fireplace to hear the next instalment of *Robinson Crusoe*. We listened, a year out from the hospital stay, to a recording of Elizabeth Bishop, husky and matter-of-fact, reading 'Crusoe in England' to a live audience in 1974.

There are other ways that I find language wobblier these days. The conversation between me and Hans has been nothing like I thought it would be, nothing like that grand correspondence between Lowell and Hardwick. When it came to actually breaking up, which we did at my insistence, we had to learn a new language, while resisting the temptation to lapse back into the one that had served us well to speak of childcare, taxes, holiday plans. Now that we have time to address anything we like, it's difficult to remember what we might have wanted to talk about on all those nights and days we did not have, all that time alone that didn't come. Talking to the people you love, letting them talk back, is much harder than anything: harder than writing this, harder than naming all the feelings. Hardwick and Lowell do well, but then Lowell's poems are published, spiked with that dialogue he dreamed up in his head; and Hardwick's fury after their publication opens up a long period of silence between them.

If Shannon had died, or not got better, I might still have written about her. It remains one of my great pleasures to think of her from a distance. To think of them all, actually. Sometimes I sit and do just that. My feet up, my mind turned over to love-thinking, I imagine Marie coming up the path on her bike, her head tipped towards me at that angle of impatience she has, the smile on her face as she tells me where she is going off to study; Rohan sleeping like a starfish in his bed, or flinging his small body into the cold Baltic sea, gathering the bravado he will need as a teenager in this blighted world. It's easy to love them. But sometimes the dialogue feels overwhelming.

I know I must give Hans this manuscript to read. Levin ends *Anna Karenina* wondering whether he should try and explain to Kitty the great revelation he's had about the universe being accessible only in small acts of kindness. He decides to say nothing and turns, instead, to go as Kitty has asked him and check on the preparation of the guest room. Importantly, though, his love for the baby is becoming a dialogue: *Mitya, that day, obviously, unquestionably, had begun to recognize his own people.*

CHAPTER SEVEN

LOVE OF THE CHILD

In August 2019, four months after the stroke, I took Rohan to America. Shannon was out of the clinic she'd been transferred to from the London hospital, and back in her apartment by then. She was walking up the stairs, beginning to move around the city. The people who'd stayed close to her since she got out of rehab were leaving her on her own more often. I'd spent most of the summer catching up on my Danish job and moving into my own place, setting up routines as a single parent with the kids. When Marie and Rohan were with Hans, I flew as often as I could between Copenhagen and the US. There was plenty of loss to reckon with, but the fact that Shannon had escaped death glazed everything in the sweet, hard fact of life. Everywhere I found evidence that some kind of living must, and could, continue.

Rohan was good-humoured on the flight to New York, open to whatever adventure I was about to deliver. When we landed in Newark he noted the language of Hollywood flowing from the posters and screens, splashed across the hotel lobby. He was nine now, a long way from being the baby I once hustled through the Detroit airport. In recent years, movies and books had given him a vivid picture of America.

We stayed that night at the same Newark hotel that Shannon had taken me to in February. This time, without sex to think of, I observed things closely as Rohan pointed them out: the ice machine, the elevator, the complicated remote control for the television. He slept beside me, russet hair damp on the white pillow, quiet with exhaustion. I felt a love for him so different from romance – a closeness that came with being in charge, entrusted with getting a smaller and more vulnerable body through the night.

It is not easy to give children the agency they deserve in a narrative focused, at least until now, on the vicissitudes of adult life. The feelings of adults for each other may change and falter, but the devotion children warrant is meant to be of a steadier kind. I have thought about my own childhood often these last years: the way my brothers and I were privy to my parents' dramas in the 1970s and 80s; the agency we felt, and lacked, in relation to their love lives. In *Monkey Grip* and *The Waterfall* and *Doctor Zhivago* the children are loved – but they have no role in actually shaping the story. This was not true of Rohan and Marie, who shaped what we did. But it is also the case that I sometimes wanted to claim the larger view for myself, and to hold them more stoically in sight.

The months after Rohan was born were difficult. Hans had signed up enthusiastically to take parental leave from his Danish job, but not until four months after the birth. I had some time off from teaching in the US, but I still needed to finish a book if I wanted to keep my job. Everything I had been working on before the birth sat on my desk, abandoned in exhaustion, trumped by my curiosity about the wakeful baby who was always with me now. When I was away from him, it was hard to sit anywhere without wanting to lay my head on my arms and rest. When we were together, I spent afternoons pushing the pram around the damp paths of Christianshavn, trying to ward off my own state of physical dereliction and make him sleep – just not too much. In the evenings I nursed him in bed with a book propped lightly on his hip. One of the novels I read in that state was Penelope Fitzgerald's *Offshore*, which reminded me, even with Rohan's infant fingers exploring the crevices of my softened body, how soon those literal points of attachment would end.

Offshore focuses on Nenna, a single mother living with her two children in a barge on the Thames. Fitzgerald writes with slight nostalgia about that setting. From the perspective of 1979, when *Offshore* won the Booker Prize, the river community of the 1960s seems like a site of incipient loss. The barge owners include a male prostitute, an aged painter, an unhappily married businessman, all gathered together on the water that runs alongside the shambles of the Holloway Road. Lovely, poor and indecisive about her marriage to a man who will not move with her onto the barge, Nenna asserts her independence by sticking to the river. Her barge floats more securely than some of the others, but her parenting is, by most standards, lacklustre. She stays up late with her neighbours, lets twelve-year old Martha skip school and make dinner for her precocious six-year-old sister, Tilda, and the two children are often left to roam freely around London.

Unlike *Monkey Grip* or *The Waterfall* – those other novels describing single motherhood in that era of my own childhood – *Offshore* follows the kids well out of Nenna's orbit, tracking the way they see the world when they are left alone in it. Martha flirts with a boy; Tilda climbs the mast of a boat like a solitary cat and gets sized up by a local criminal. At one point the two of them go hunting for hand-painted Victorian tiles that fell long ago from a capsized boat and have been lodged ever since in the river's mud. The girls collect them when the sun is at an angle low enough to illuminate the shallows. Martha spies the old ceramic gleaming in the light and directs Tilda, in her rubber boots, to fish the bright squares from the water. They take their small haul to an untrustworthy antique dealer, and Martha, knowing a little of the tiles' value, drives the price high enough to fund the purchase of Cliff Richard records at Woolworths.

Offshore brought back to me the figure of my mother, waiflike and desirable, caught in the drift of male attention, swimming to rescue the dog; open to life and the new setting of Australia, but slow to apply the kinds of parental attention that middle-class life is meant to involve. Days with her and my father as single parents, both working low-wage jobs, showed me how it felt to be a child alone with my experiences, though not unloved or entirely unseen. Like Nenna, my parents put little emphasis on us getting dressed or avoiding dangerous places. They saw that I skipped school, and worried about it. But they also wanted my brothers and stepsisters and me to be out in the world, caring for ourselves, breaking the rules. My father played Pink Floyd's 'Another Brick in the Wall' regularly and encouraged us to sing along. In *Offshore*, Tilda and Martha serve as witnesses to the sexuality and sadness of adults, but Fitzgerald also gives them chapters of their own, daring us to see things from their point of view.

Good novels about children can make youth a prism through which to show adult lives as mysterious, alien scripts. It will take a lifetime for Stephen Dedalus, the child sung to on his father's knee in James Joyce's *Portrait of the Artist as a Young Man*, to decode the puzzling lines of the story he is told there: *there was a moocow coming down along the road and this moocow that was coming down along the road met a nicens little boy named baby tuckoo.* It's by putting himself into those lines, telling it back to himself, that Stephen begins to make sense of it: *His father told him that story: his father looked at him through a glass: he had a hairy face. He was baby tuckoo.*

My childhood was riddled with moments in which I felt outside the frame of the story and struggled to put myself into it. Hearing 'Frère Jacques' sung at my new Australian kindergarten, I understood the line *Sonnez les matines* as being about me – *sunny little Tina.* Or there was the time when my mother threw up in a taxi and said helplessly to the driver, *I have been sick. Yes,* I agreed silently, *beans can do that to you. I do not like beans, either.* Language is not always generous. It can produce a wasteland of misunderstandings, a long corridor of closed doors along which the child knocks many times on the wrong one before anyone answers.

Henry James's *What Maisie Knew* describes a divorce with shocking cruelty. It is told from the perspective of Maisie, a child tossed between her upper-class parents, who are bent on doing each other harm. Few children in fiction have it harder than she does, while trying to interpret the bad behaviour she is seeing and hearing. Lost in a maze of adult animosities, Maisie tries to make sense of the world through language. When she is with her father, his friends perch her on their knees, fondling her matchstick legs. She puzzles over the pinching of her calves as they search for something to which *her nurse gave a short, ugly name, a name painfully associated with the part of the joint, at dinner, that she didn't like.* 'Fat', that word she cannot say, haunts her as she thinks about her legs in relation to those of other children. Words are no help at all in describing what is happening in her parents' outrageous new love lives, where she remains a mere instrument, *a ready vessel for bitterness.* Names for people change and slide around even when Maisie thinks she has them in her grasp. She calls Miss Overmore her governess, until she becomes her father's new wife, Mrs Farange. Then she calls Sir Claude her stepfather, until it becomes clear that he's no longer her mother's lover. Much to the horror of her nurse, Maisie names the other men – *Mr Perriam? Lord Eric?* – who might be her next stepfathers, insinuating herself by way of those risky words into the realm of adult gossip. I remember trying, like that, to get my mother to believe I understood things beyond my ken. *Is he good in bed?* I asked once, trying without success to enter the inner circle of her intimate life. *No, actually*, she replied. At the end of the novel Maisie is on a ship drifting away from them all, the misdemeanours of adults piling up in the rear-view mirror, her precocious punt on inclusion at its end.

Offshore and *What Maisie Knew* are adult stories in which children get to be protagonists, at least in the sense that we see what they see much of the time. I would like to be able to give you Marie and Rohan's very different points of view. In the last years they have had to contend with as much adult feeling and vocabulary as Maisie. But I do not know exactly what those days when I was alone in Sweden with my thoughts of Shannon were like for them, or the ones when I sat at her side in her hospital ward, flying back to Copenhagen to weep and sleep in gloom. It's an effort to imagine the weeks Rohan and Marie have spent alone with Hans in his grief, or the way they are becoming part of his new Danish life now, populated by people I've never met. But I know how many words and concepts have floated Rohan's way as part of this rearrangement. 'Gay', he likes to say backwards: *Yag stuff. Are you guys talking again about yag ffuts? Is he yag oot?* If I try, I can imagine him joking with his friends, who ask what it's all been like. Who is that short-haired American he loves now? Who is his mother?

Taking Rohan to meet Shannon that first time was an important moment of unity between us. Waking very early beside him at the airport hotel, I felt the possibility of introducing him to places I'd been since Shannon's stroke. I also felt properly attuned for the first time in many months to his way of looking. We went early from the Newark hotel into New York, watched squirrels in Washington Square, lingered at a playground full of babysitters and their charges. Braving the heat, we shopped for Pokémon cards and ate sushi while he sorted them out in an air-conditioned café. On the Amtrak train to Philadelphia a few days later, I tried to find out how much Rohan understood. *Yes*, he said, he understood that Shannon was my girlfriend now, and was fine with that as long as there was no *kissing at night. Yes*, he knew how sick she'd been, *but could she still come to the movies? To the game shop?* In the end she did those things valiantly on wobbly legs, and Rohan drank it all in – not the American life he'd read about, but life nonetheless.

One of the accusations that Queer Theory has levelled most directly against straight people is that they are too invested in children. Writing in 2004, the critic Lee Edelman argues that the figurative child haunts heterosexual American culture, a promise of a particular kind of future that must be protected. That imaginary child *seems to shimmer with the iridescent promise of Noah's rainbow, serving like the rainbow as the pledge of a covenant that shields us against the persistent threat of ... now. No Future* is a dazzling piece of argumentation on behalf of queer presentism. It shows that our very sense of momentum involves ceding the present to the imaginary figure of the unborn child, writing letters and novels to her in our own minds. Sex without reproduction becomes a form of death, the family part of a larger structure that drains off libidinal energies by configuring them as an investment in the generation to come. Edelman's right in many ways, of course. But I think he's especially right when it comes to the habits of characters. Elizabeth and Darcy hardly get to enjoy Pemberley before the question of having children looms. If Will and James could somehow get together in *The Swimming Pool Library*, they would inevitably adopt that precious nephew Roops, who hovers in the wings as a charming man-child.

What makes me less convinced by Edelman is my sense of how many loud arguments were made in the 1970s by real, straight people against the family, the preciousness of the child. Why on earth, argued Germaine Greer, would you want to live in a unit of four when a larger unit could provide cooking and childcare, when children collectively tended could give parents the freedom to come and go as they wanted? Why, asked Suzanne Brøgger, imagining the small-town Danish postman on his yellow bike, would a single person who could easily earn enough to live on, and still have plenty of time for pleasure and education, want to sign up for a more expensive life in which the parent is expected to sacrifice himself for new appliances and school fees? The authors read by my parents and their friends protested against children becoming idols in whose name jobs and marriages were endured, mortgages stretched, travel or sex deferred. They moved to Australia motivated to pursue a certain kind of radical life, rather than delay it. During that season of the bearded philosopher, the Take Back the Night marches, the naked swimming evenings, I was surrounded – like Martha and Tilda – by adults living more energetically than full-time childcare allowed. The people around me believed, like Edelman, that a larger community and a fully realised present were more important than the future of the abstract child. In this context, we were the mascots for our parents' rejection of bourgeois forms of life. The prints for which my friend Jonah's mother became well known show young boys looking wild and strong, their freckled boldness highlighted in red and orange paint in the silkscreen studio, light streaming down from an aqua-tinted sky. We were there, running around naked in the gardens and on the heaths, going to country schools and staying up late – hardly a reason to defer pleasure.

My parents were dedicated to their moment, their own

generation. But they also had a strong sense of the natural world that came from an earlier time and another place. My mother grew up in rural Scotland, went to boarding school in St Andrews and spent a year in a remote corner of the Lake Distract recovering from a bad LSD trip that she had at Oxford. Her vivid sense of that landscape's recuperative powers chimes with lines of Romantic poetry, plump Cumberland clouds, lush hillsides and mountain clefts enfolding wistful walkers and presciently wise infants. Suckled on daffodil milk, Wordsworth's children delight in meadows and groves, leap in delight in their mothers' arms, harvest flowers and cluster around their siblings in unity. I know my mother was thinking of all that when she chose Australia. In *Letters Written in Sweden*, Wollstonecraft sails with two-year-old Fanny to the edge of the world and stands in the presence of Nordic mountains and shores, imagining with horror a planet becoming too populated. Two centuries before my parents emigrated to a continent they knew next to nothing about, radical adults were dreaming of taking children out of the city and allowing them to roam free.

The Australian bush was nothing like the Lake District, of course. The bearded philosopher argued in essays he wrote in favour of the phenomenological specificity of a harsh and stolen land. When he took Jonah and me to his campsite in the dunes, he sent us out to play while he sorted and chopped wood, and read, and opened cans for dinner. Wandering far from camp, we followed pelicans and hunted for baby rabbits. A few days into one of those trips I had my cheek pressed against the leaves of succulent plants, one arm deep inside a burrow and another braced on the surface of the sand, when Jonah hit my hand hard with a hatchet. I didn't cry until we'd pulled the blade from between my tendons and the blood began to spill upwards in lazy spurts. It took four hours to drive to the closest doctor. Jonah held my arm up while the philosopher sang songs about bushrangers and bandits. The evening air whistled through the open sides of the jeep and I felt the adventure coming into focus around me, hoping there would be people I could tell this bloody story to.

The most terrifying prospect in *What Maisie Knew* is that there will be no witness to the child's existence, only a narrator who lends her temporary visibility and then leaves her alone in a world she does not understand. To the self-serving adults around her, Maisie's confusion is sweet, her small victories of comprehension the tricks of a circus animal. She is used and easily dispensed with. Trapped in a universe where evil, cake for tea, and sheer negligence carry the equal weight that only a child can give them, she will never see the light. She will not recalibrate her views or understand in the end what has happened. Maisie's childhood is more haunting for this reason than the ones David Copperfield and Jane Eyre and Stephen Dedalus narrate. They may have been abused and neglected, shoved into slimy ditches at school, left to fend for themselves in uncaring institutions, but they grew up to reconcile those experiences with adult perspectives, retelling their loneliness in language they have mastered and put to work. Even Frankie Addams of *The Member of the Wedding* seems set to attain the consciousness of the one who tells this story about her twelve-year-old tomboy self. But Maisie is not primed to become a narrator. She will never grow up, or understand, or have anyone listen to her side of the story.

It is the most terrible prospect to me that the adventures of the children I love should remain unreconciled with the larger account of these last years that I am giving. I am haunted by the parts of my own childhood that had no mature witnesses; by the days with Jonah that shake down too easily into stories of us untended, playing like Tilda and Martha on the fringes of adult lives. Hans, who grew up in northern Germany in the 1970s, has only slightly less sinister stories of roaming the forests around Hamburg with axes and arrows and fireworks. Shannon has pictures of herself as a three-year-old in the desert, hair tangled, beer cans in the background, the camera barely trained on her. And yet all of us were, I think, heard in the end by our adults, and encouraged to share our side of things. We were seen, however haphazardly, in our specificity, and had stories told to and about us. There were many witnesses in the end to my wounded hand – adults to admire my rows of stitches, to praise Jonah's bravery in pulling out the hatchet and holding the flaps of skin together during the long drive.

My plea for the parenting that I got and for the parenting I have done lies largely, as a positive iteration of Edelman's argument might suggest, in the importance of making the most of the time we have. It is true, my own happiness may have featured more largely than the happiness of mothers is meant to, over these last years. But Hans and I always tried – even before things took this turn, even after Marie was born – to live adult life to the full. Edelman's account of the figurative child as a tyrant preventing such behaviour does not take much interest in low-key sites of everyday rebellion. But Hans and I always let the kids play in the building sites of our lives. They've gone to Danish institutions, ambitious in collective rather than individual terms, and to inner-London schools as members of a white minority. They've been sent off in the countryside and told to swim and roam and chop wood; and they've been witness to love affairs that have done them no obvious good. But they have also been talked into existence by multiple adults who treat them, even when they have gone to bed, as the most interesting characters of all – the ones to follow most closely in any novel where they might appear. A community of opinions tends generously towards the young. Of Mitya, Kitty and his nurse share theories about his intelligence and beauty. Having such a consensus rigged in your favour can make being a child bearable.

As an adult, I have frequently accused my mother of depriving me of the opportunities for good company and class identity that would have come if she'd worked, like her Oxford peers, as a journalist or an economist or a therapist in England; instead she moved to a setting where she has been, and remains, a cleaner, a sorter of mail, a blazer of rural trails, a person pitied sometimes by her co-workers for the long stints her children have spent in education. I've snorted at her insinuations that it wasn't that easy – that they believed back then in something more than the fate of the single human being. I've forgotten at times how many of the books I read belonged first to my parents.

At other times I too have insisted, like them, that my kids were not special causes, not beings for which adult happiness or collective living should be sacrificed. But if I consider the stories read aloud, the classics chosen for them, the pride taken in Marie and Rohan's ability to drink in ideas, I have without doubt been a purveyor of the cultural capital that stands them now in good stead. In *Light Years*, Viri confesses in relation to bedtime stories that he wants his children to have two lives: *an old life and a new life, a life that is indivisible from all lives past, that grows from them, exceeds them, and another that is original, pure, free, that is beyond the prejudice which protects us, the habit which gives us shape.* In this context, he checks himself for reading to them of *woodcutters* and *honest fishermen*, filling their days with puppet shows and pictures, exemplary parental conversations that will no doubt lead to college applications.

Asked once by a Danish talk-show host what we could do to make kids read more, I fumbled, thinking too long about the premises of the question. Why *do* we want them to read more fiction? It's not a script for how to live that we are offering them, in the form of Victorian novels and boarding-school tales. If we take out of the equation the efforts of a class trying to reproduce itself, what are we left with? Perhaps Viri is right, and it has something to do with the originality that lies in the difference between the old story and the new, the way in which everything might still be reread if only it stays in circulation. I do believe in the novel supporting a world other than the one that is, and in this difference being what matters. The Romantics wanted that originality for their children. Wollstonecraft wished nothing more for the toddler she took to Scandinavia than a world where women were free, as she was not. Fanny killed herself in the end but her half-sister, Mary, whose birth killed Wollstonecraft, grew up to write *Frankenstein*, a testament – if ever there was one – to new things emerging from old.

In the novels Rohan likes best, the world is in great peril. There is a hero involved, usually a young man destined to confront an enemy of innumerable strength. The hero discovers his powers, developing and guarding them from general knowledge, growing up in the face of danger to become the one person who can save everyone from bitter destruction. Rohan has hunted these stories down in bookshops around the world, series after series of books like this; worshipping teenage characters who win their battles against aliens, hostile gods, vengeful magi, invading armies, who fight to the death in competitions for survival. I have been a little scathing about his taste for that plot, a distant spin-off from those early novels of Defoe, pitting the individual against a hostile world. Yet there is something I understand about the appeal in this literature of stories of rescue and redemption.

After our week in Philadelphia, Rohan and I went back and spent a few more days in New York. The temperature was already dangerously high that summer, and I splurged on a room in a downtown hotel with a pool. Rohan lay there on a white plastic lounger in an inner courtyard shaded by ferns, curled into me with a towel over his head, and finished a novel called *Storm Thief*. He was happy, but he was also reading novels the way I once did: undercover, deep at night, crumpling with despair when the last volume of a series ended. *Call the author*, he demanded when he finished a series, *and make him write the sequel now*. The stories that absorbed him on that trip did little to promote the humanist version of survival and recovery that I wanted to deliver. But they prepared him well for many kinds of disaster that have come to pass: this quiet pandemic, police brutality, the seas rising.

Children's books are worth considering as evidence of what children actually like. But they rarely help with the perfectly ordinary subject of one's parent finding a new love. In so many classics, the loss of the family seems worse than the end of the world. The father in jail in *The Railway Children*, parents dead in *The Secret Garden*, children forced to fend for themselves in an old favourite of my mine, *Baby Island*, where teenage girls are shipwrecked with four babies and a mysterious supply of talc and nappies. *The Endless Steppe*, which I ordered through the school book club and relished in a cheap edition that smelt of newly cut paper, recounts the deportation during the Second World War of a well-off Polish girl and her family to Siberia. Esther, more adaptable than her parents and grandparents, must survive by making clothes for the Russians in exchange for potatoes and cabbage. At Rohan's age, I liked fictional children to be alone enough to experience their agency, but able to count on the family as a safety net. If the presence of parents was too conspicuous, the freedom of children felt false. I did not submit fully to *Swallows and Amazons*, where the proximity of the island to the mainland means that food and help are suspiciously close at hand; and where John, the teenage captain, is so clearly a stand-in for the absent father he needs to please. Yet I desperately wanted the family unit to survive. I felt my body tremble and sigh each time I read that Roberta was united with her father at the end of *The Railway Children*.

In those righteous stories where the family must be saved, it's not enough for a child to fight the enemy. The bigger point is to keep a small group on the raft as the flood comes in and washes everyone else away. There is no happy ending unless the family makes it out together. More important than saving a world is the fact that children are protected by parents united as a team. In Laura Ingalls Wilder's *The Long Winter*, the family huddles through weeks of heavy snow inside a small house in an outpost in Dakota. They twist straw into fuel that can be burned and watch their supplies dwindle. When things get desperate, Pa goes out on his horse into the storm and returns with supplies of grain that he has forced an unmarried settler to relinquish. The story ends, like all instalments of *Little House on the Prairie*, with Christmas, the point in time and space where the ending and the desire to be together as part of a family align perfectly.

It's easy to critique these kinds of stories, especially with an argument like Edelman's in mind. Why should the frontier settler in *The Long Winter* not get to save his seeds, plant his crop, flourish as he'd planned? Maybe he'd have founded a better community, one more inclusive of outsiders. Maybe he'd have adopted children. Historically, it's anyway the *papoosed* babies Laura sees in that landscape that we should be watching out for. How could Ma and Pa have really been happy in roles so circumscribed by gender? Surely there are things Ma wants that are not even visible here; countless ways in which it would be better if everyone in the town waited out the storm together rather than being penned into their tiny houses and the *mini-families* Brøgger despises. But Pa's diverting of resources into the mouths of his children at Christmas follows a logic that is hard to shake. I've had many friends steeped in queer and feminist theory ask me in serious voices how my children are doing. *How will we handle Christmas?*

It's not as if I haven't worried myself over how to save children from the dangers of the world that roar to life without the family as protection. For a few years after Rohan was born, I had nightmares that involved trying to rescue two children at risk of drowning: huge waves crashed over us – me, Marie and the baby at sea. The problem was how to pluck them both from the water, how to get them both to land. Having a second child opened up my fear of being unable to care for the first, a sense of us being a group that needed saving from the world. The nightmare went away at one point, after a holiday on the island of Mull when Rohan was four. Hans and I were there with the kids, my mother and stepfather. Marie and Rohan played in rockpools and on sandbars, walked into caves, searched for otters. Rohan had a stuffed toy that he took everywhere with him. One day at low tide we took the children picnicking on an outcrop of rocky land across the damp sand, and lolled around together like a family of seals in a dell while the warm sun got lower. When the tide turned, the water rose fast and we found ourselves almost cut off from the shore. Marie bravely tied her shoes together and slung them over her shoulder, gathered things into her arms; and Hans piggybacked Rohan and his stuffed toy through the strong-flowing inlet. We were up to our waists in sea with bags on our heads. It was the closest I'd come to the dark scenario of my dreams, but I was laughing at us all being in it together and making it out the other side.

Pandemic days have left me dreaming again of life rafts, discombobulated once more on this subject of survival, my loyalties split and scattered. Rohan with a bad cough. Is it my job to look after him or keep him away from Shannon, who is still tired and full of anti-stroke medicine; away from Marie, who has her exams to take? Maybe I am meant to keep all of us, including Hans, sequestered from the rest of the world, which is full of people more vulnerable to death than us, but also a source of potential infection and competition over resources. Perhaps the problem is less the desire to keep small bodies above the waterline, than the limited version of that instinct. But it is unclear if there are family rafts big enough to hold everyone. I was always critical of that documentary about male penguins left to guard their eggs from the bitter cold while the females go off actively in search of food. From a feminist perspective, it is heartening that the father penguins stay home and huddle. The mood of the documentary swells as the camera shows the mothers returning weeks later, and just in time, spewing regurgitated fish into the beaks of a hungry chick, which they magically recognise as their own. The flaw is that while some female penguins never come back and some chicks never hatch, no mother with a full gullet ever adopts a chick not biologically her own.

If parenting and family were more loosely defined, all those stories of peril and salvation might be better. Imlay never did come to Fanny's rescue, but William Godwin brought her up after Wollstonecraft died giving birth to Mary. Lowell may have left Harriet under Hardwick's care in New York, but he became – by accounts other than his own – an excellent stepfather to Caroline Blackwood's daughters in England. Moll Flanders found biological ties an encumbrance, but she was loyal to the substitute families she created in her travels around the world. My mother has loved many children and young adults well enough, taken pride in grandchildren whose genes are not her own. In the end, on that trip to Philadelphia, it was Shannon who distracted Rohan from his books of conflict and disaster with Marvel movies and microwave popcorn, artificial substances on which it seemed possible to feed whole empires.

Rohan and I got back from New York in time for the start of the Danish school term. On evenings at my sublet flat, surrounded by the furniture of another family, we read Ursula Le Guin's *Earthsea Trilogy* aloud and drew maps together of imaginary worlds, Skyping Shannon to show her the bridges and oceans and forests we had imagined. Rohan seemed fine in the day, but he often fell asleep in my bed at night, teary about his life being broken into parts. Marie came and went, angry in her own way about the inconvenience of it all, unimpressed with my offerings of smoothies and tired chat. I worked until I was exhausted and woke early, setting the alarm, stealing from the tail end of the night the hours in which I first started to write this book. It was not a way to fix things but, like those drawings I did with Rohan, it was something to do while the healing happened.

Many authors have confronted a crisis in parenting by writing about it. If the paradox of writing about marriage is that it involves a structural kind of betrayal – an intimacy of the narrator and reader that belies the claims of the story – the paradox of stories about parenting is that writing about the children you love entails being, in one way or another, away from them. This predicament is one of the jokes at the heart of Laurence Sterne's *Tristram Shandy*, a sensationally popular and funny fictional autobiography, published in nine volumes from the late 1750s. The narrative, ostensibly, is the one of Tristram's life, and it begins with his parents' diligent efforts to produce a child. The humour of the novel lies largely in the comparison between the idiosyncratic misfit of a man that Tristram so evidently is, and the efforts of his parents to engineer this perfect being. Walter, his father, believes that the moment of conception is key to a child's character and focuses hard on the implanting of a small being inside the womb. His mother, who is less interested in the sex, focuses more on being taken to London to lie-in and be attended by a midwife. Tristram's father, a bookish learner, explores more modern options: Caesarean section, male midwives, forceps-assisted delivery. He hopes that science will protect the infant's brain from the feckless female body, but is also open to the old magic of words, believing that his favourite name, Trismegistus, will save the ill-born baby from the accidents that have befallen him. But by the age of six, Tristram has been misnamed, has had his foreskin snipped off by a falling window and has learned more than any child needs to about the sex life of his uncle next door. As adult narrator, his lusts, vanities and dissipations are on show as an illustration of how wrong parenting by the book can go.

The travesty is that while Tristram's childhood unfolds in a spirit of disaster and accident, Walter Shandy is occupied with writing the *Tristrapaedia*, a systematic account of every-thing he has learned about child-raising. His research and writing mean that he misses every practical chance he might have had to shape Tristram's opinions. Whatever kind of man Tristram is, whatever strange movements of his heart and brain we follow, Walter's writings run parallel to this reality without being of any real consequence to his upbring-ing. The irony extends to the fact that Tristram is writing his own book now – the one we are reading – and that it too risks being an alternative to living, a long treatise on the things he thinks and feels, whose production prevents him from having to act on any of them.

Sterne illuminates a paradox that all real and fictional autobiographers have to face in representing life as something from which hours and weeks, and even years, of writing must ultimately be subtracted. But this equation grows more acute when there are children to be cared for. Karl Ove Knausgård's six-volume autofiction, *My Struggle*, stages this confronta-tion with a candour that twenty-first-century readers have welcomed. With a dedication to self-observation as acute as Tristram's, Knausgård tracks his life back to the moments of his 1970s childhood in Norway, while reflecting in the present tense on his practices and ambitions as a writer, and on the circulation of his novels among his readers. The child-hood he remembers in many ways resembles mine. Children play and cycle, and masturbate into bottles in the woods; grow up in the custody of parents who have moved out of the city, gone back to university, betrayed each other, separ-ated. It's a childhood of intense reading – hours of the child being immobilised with a book. Karl Ove loves *The Earthsea*

Trilogy, knowing as soon as he opens the first one that it will be good.

Knausgård also writes in detail about the time he spends with his own children. The second volume of his novel, *A Man in Love*, documents closely the months he stays at home with his baby daughter while wanting to write. *Autumn passed into winter, life with baby food and baby clothes, and baby cries and baby vomit, utterly wasted mornings and empty afternoons began to take their toll, but I couldn't complain, couldn't say anything, I just had to keep my mouth shut and do what I had to do.* Living as a foreigner in Sweden, where parental leave is well paid and shared, the first years of his success as a writer overlap with those in which he learns to negotiate his time and his masculinity under these conditions: ranging the city with children in a pram, occupying the sidelines at kids' birthday parties, taking road trips with infants. There was nothing particularly surprising about any of these descriptions to my friends, who read Knausgård with enthusiasm. But the publicity accruing to all this challenge of combining writing and parenting felt new, as if in the hands of a man the problems were coming for the first time into the spotlight.

That basic friction between the need to write about parenting and the everyday labour of doing it has stayed prominent in autofiction ever since. It drives the work of Rachel Cusk, Maggie Nelson, Jenny Offill, Sophie Ratcliffe. After the birth of her son, Nelson contemplates the bubble into which she might just disappear. Pragmatically she insists, *I feel no urge to extricate myself from this bubble. But here's the catch: I cannot hold my baby at the same time as I write.* Fair enough. Even Wollstonecraft did not write with Fanny literally at her side. She took a nanny along with her on her trip to Sweden, and she left the two alone for six weeks when the journey north became too arduous. Wordsworth almost certainly never cooked or washed for the children he wrote about. Lowell, committed in the 1970s to recounting his daily life with stepchildren, depended on an army of night-nurses, summer camps, boarding schools. In New York, Hardwick worried about Harriet and her grades and diets, but Lowell shut the door to his study and forgot everything so practical as he sat down to write about his newly extended family. The philosopher, on the other hand, was really there with us, making dinner, lighting the fire. His camp had a folding table and a chair. Had he not had Jonah and me with him, our bodies hungry and disobedient and prone to injury, he might have written of the future from that bright perspective of the 1970s.

Knausgård does not resolve this tension in any radical way. Thinking about Denmark now, I can say that it makes a difference to write from a society in which paid parental leave and financial support for artists and writers are generous. One shouldn't think of the parental predicament as entirely universal or individual. Greer and Brøgger were right to point to the urgent need for collective solutions. But Knausgård identifies the fact that a society where everyone is expected to do their fair share of parenting, and not to employ nannies or cleaners, has its own challenges for the parent who hopes to rewrite Proust before he is forty. Knausgård rents a studio. After his first child is born, he vanishes into it for many weeks, dedicates himself to the writing process at the exclusion of all reason. His wife, who also wants to make art, calls him in despair, reminds him he has a baby now, but Knausgård writes on, ignoring her pleas and threats. When she says he should consider himself single – that she's left him – he keeps writing. He finishes the novel on exactly the day he has promised it to his publisher.

I know how it feels to part ways with children in your care for weeks at a time in order to work, but I never did it in order to write about them. I left the family home to pursue a life with someone new, but not to write a book. Knausgård believes that in the end he must be an artist, and that whatever he is as a father, or a human being, will follow from that. Having never claimed that middle-of-the-day space for writing, I suppose I have claimed it now for love. On those evenings when Rohan was sad, he and I talked about New York and Shannon coming at Christmas, about how great it would be to have her in Copenhagen. And he'd cheer up and list the water parks and burger bars he wanted to show her, before asking, *Could Hans could come too?* At that point I would insist he would be glad to know me in the end, and to have me as his parent, because of all this stuff. And what Rohan said, in the darkness, was simply: *You are wrong.*

What we did agree on was *The Earthsea Trilogy*: there was a world to save, a boy needed to do it, but none of the individualism or the family ties that put me off reading Rohan's other books aloud. Ged, the lonely wizard boy, is burdened – like all of Rohan's heroes – with great skills. He trains for many years, learning in isolation the secrets of his archipelago. The power he wields in the end over dragons and demons comes down to his mastering a vocabulary for what is there. He is like Elizabeth Bishop's Crusoe: king of an island world where the singularity of things means that everything has one name, a key to its inner being; and he is like Stephen Dedalus, owning the world by learning its language better than everyone else who uses it against him.

In November, when Rohan's despair seemed greatest, he flirted with the idea that every leaf and every bottle-top on the street could be rightly or wrongly addressed. He picked flowers and put them in water, insisting that the names he had given them would keep them alive. On evening calls with Shannon and on walks with Hans, I talked constantly of him. Like that, we faced the coming of another winter.

Chapter Eight

CIRCLES OF FRIENDS

Shannon's recovery has involved many people. Her friends and family stuck around in Philadelphia that half-year after the stroke, cooked her meals, assembled furniture, covered her teaching, installed handrails in her bathroom, sat in on a new set of minor operations on her eyes, fulfilled prescriptions, researched treatments, sent playlists, read books aloud. Different people slept beside her at night, leaving their own kids and partners to be there. Each time I arrived for a visit, someone new opened the door to the building, an old factory on the shores of the Delaware. The bare rooms of that loft apartment felt flooded with care. No wonder that *Sleepless Nights*, that carefully crafted story of mid-life breakage and repair, ends with such a heartfelt invocation of Hardwick's friends: *always on the phone, always writing letters, always waking up to address myself to B. and D. and C. – those whom I dare not ring up until morning and yet must talk to throughout the night.*

Despite Hardwick's insistence on these kinds of connection, it's harder to find novels about friendship than about almost any other kind of love. Neither the steadiness of affection across the years nor the inclusive piling up of platonic loves lends itself easily to plot. While various novels feature friends – Elena Ferrante, Sally Rooney and Kazuo Ishiguro all write well about them – these fictional relationships are often constellations of enmity and competition. The relationship between Lenù and Lila drives Ferrante's *Neapolitan Quartet*, but it's often unclear whether the two women actually like each other. This is also true of the women in a novel written by Hardwick's friend, Mary McCarthy, in the 1960s. *The Group* follows eight female students graduating from Vassar College, making their way into East Coast society in 1930s America. We learn at different points over the years of these women's weddings, their furniture, their use of contraception, their parallel and sometimes interconnecting lives. Kay marries the tortured playwright Harald in the novel's opening chapter, and later invites the whole set to a party at her brightly furnished apartment. The party reveals the affair Harald is having with one of Kay's friends. A gaudy cake on a pink glass cake-stand, the offering of a loyal household help belittled for her taste, is whisked away in shame. Harald sends it down the rubbish chute and Kay rebukes him lightly, saying that it was not theirs to throw away. These people seem to know nothing of care.

The Group is ground-breaking in many ways, but it is no hymn to the kindness or constancy of relations between women. Friendships are stunted in McCarthy's rendering by rivalries, racism, infidelity, the preoccupations with status, by prejudice and jealousy. None of the characters in *The Group* represent the people McCarthy felt most warmly about at her own parties. This omission has to be reconciled with the fact that McCarthy was meticulously attentive in other areas to the world she lived in, a writer assiduously inclined to tell the truth. It was her personal dictum that *the distinctive mark of the novel is its concern with the actual world, the world of fact, of the verifiable, of figures, even, and statistics*. In general she accounts carefully for the grit of women's existence, following the money, unpacking the detail. Norman Mailer, who insulted *The Group* in a high-profile review for not being a proper novel, recognised it as a text of great sociological accuracy.

With all this truth on offer, it seems strange that McCarthy's real and fictional friendships do not align more simply with one another. The unkindness represented in the novel does not express the way McCarthy really felt about Elizabeth Bishop, who was her classmate. The one truly sovereign character in *The Group* is Lakey, who disdains the kinds of domestic and social ambition driving her classmates. She spends most of the 1930s in Europe, before reappearing at the very end of the novel with Maria, her aristocratic German lover. In her time away she's become a lesbian, which the group find generally a shame, a waste of her feminine appeal. *They tried not to think about what she and Maria did in bed together*. Their repulsion is mitigated only by the fact that Maria turns out to have a way with sewing, a sense of when to absent herself, like the best husbands, from women's gatherings. *They liked Maria as a person; if only she could have finished in a tail, like a mermaid!* If this characterisation were simply sociological, Lakey and Maria would be a match with Bishop and Lota. Bishop herself feared this might be the case and she accused McCarthy of the unkind likeness. But McCarthy insisted that this resemblance had never crossed her mind. She hadn't been thinking of Bishop at all; her feelings for her friend were utterly different from the censorial ones that the younger, fictional group feels for its lesbian outlier.

The reality of friendship slips through the net of *The Group*'s descriptive reckoning partly because of its historical slant. McCarthy was looking back harshly on the 1930s. Perhaps it did take thirty years for those young women to leave betrayal and competition behind them and form real collaborations and post-divorce configurations. It would be nice to think that women being friends became easier in the 1960s than it had been in the 1930s. Yet this does not solve the puzzle of how those kinder and more sustainable feelings – the ones the real McCarthy had for the real Bishop – would show up in a novel where an author wanted to honour them. There's no real friendship between women in *The Waterfall* or *Offshore*. Is there any fictional register in which McCarthy could have represented a friendship like the close one she had for twenty-five years with the philosopher Hannah Arendt, over decades during which both women were successful writers involved in current and literary events? Their international lives took them on lecture tours and journalistic engagements, grand tours and sojourns. Arendt wrote to McCarthy when she was in Aberdeen as the first woman ever to give the prestigious Gifford Lectures; Mary wrote from Saigon, where she covered the Vietnam War, and from Paris, where she wrote urbane essays and reviews for the *New York Review of Books*, and from the many trips she took with the last of her four husbands. The friends defended each other through the publication of Arendt's controversial coverage of the Eichmann trial and the successful reception of *The Group*; they holidayed together, consoled each other for lost loves, stayed long in each other's spacious apartments.

Arendt and McCarthy's letters to each other are sometimes political. More often they record them performing ordinary rites of affection: sending birthday flowers, expensive pieces of jewellery; planning airport pickups, fussing over hotel bookings; advice about hair; requesting the forwarding of dental supplies left behind in a spare room in New York. They comment critically on Lowell's bad behaviour in publishing *The Dolphin*, and appreciatively of Hardwick's blooming after her divorce from him; and of Sartre's arrogance, the way he had Beauvoir and all of France at his command. McCarthy describes how she has squirmed with discomfort when composing *The Group*'s sex scenes, imagining Arendt's disapproval of all that intimate American detail. Yet Arendt declares the novel brilliant, loves the way McCarthy exculpates herself from its more damning scenes, deems it worthy of all the money it earns. McCarthy's eulogy for Arendt describes the beauty of her body in motion: the turn of her ankles, the animation of her hands, the brilliance of her mind. After the funeral, McCarthy began to work with the notes Arendt had left behind, turning them into her last book. Friendship structures these two real lives as a form of intelligence and literary output that surmounts and absorbs the many phases of other relationships they live through. The very steadiness and lack of guile in McCarthy and Arendt's relationship distinguishes it from those represented in *The Group*, where no connection between women is so happy or constant or unscarred by male love interests.

When I think of the friends I have kept over the years, I am left like Hardwick, with B and D and C in my mind as the people I will call up or write to once this page is done. It feels good to conjure them up: C in her new house, B taking his daughter to school, D delivering her lecture to the crowd. Their faces are points of light in the dark climate of my imagination, growing brighter over time. That passionate friendship with Imogen ended abruptly when I left for the US, and it was messy to begin with. But I like to think a novel could be written about those particular days in Brighton when her company was a source of deep joy to me, something larger than myself, its own point of fulfilment. Just going to a movie or sitting on our sagging sofa, joking with her, could make me happier than anything.

The literary scenes to match that feeling are scattered without plotlines across pages shaped by romance and intrigue. Jane Eyre is coaxed out of trauma by her school friend, the older, wiser and otherworldly Helen Burns. Helen sits on the ground beside Jane as she sobs. Putting her arms around her own knees and resting her head there, Helen offers her body as a sign of human solidarity in the desert of Lowood School. At the end of *The Magic Mountain*, Mann zooms in on the relation between the cousins Joachim and Castorp, which has seemed until now almost coincidental to the themes of the novel. Joachim dies in the sanatorium, although he wants desperately to fight in the war, while Castorp, who would sooner have opted out of history, goes back into the world. But they find each other when Joachim is dying, and Castorp grieves genuinely for his cousin's company. There is something about the affection between the two men in the end

– the ordinary soldier and the civilian – that pushes back against the necessity of war. It is a moment akin to the night that Vivaldo and Eric spend together in *Another Country*, or to the other ones in Baldwin's fiction where friends connect deeply without hoping for anything from that communion. These deeply befriended characters seem to wait for a story to sustain them, a future that will allow them to keep living together. It is a wait that seems longer for those in the novel than in real life. Perhaps, to put this in temporal terms, there are few novels long enough for friendship – no fictional time stretched sufficiently to capture friendship as the one kind of love that prevails over others. Although Lenù and Lila do not always champion each other, at least the four volumes of the *Neapolitan Quartet* give them the space to lose and find each other many times.

During the months Shannon was being cared for in Philadelphia, and Rohan and I were reading *A Wizard of Earthsea*, my mother and stepfather came to visit Copenhagen. They were on their way to stay in the Lake District with a group of my mother's schoolmates from boarding school. In the last few years my mother's life has been full of people. With money enough from her small government pension for travel, she has reconnected to the landscapes and circles of her childhood. Although she remains a cleaner and a cheese-seller in South Australia, her life there is one of walking groups and circles of people petitioning the council on environmental causes. That dusty country town where I spent my lonely teenage years has become an oasis of yoga studios and health-food co-operatives, populated by alternative people whose well-intentioned lives have become stable in the end.

On that visit to Copenhagen my mother was full of disapproval about the turn my life had taken. She stayed at my new flat and drank tea with Hans in our old one. My life and children seemed to her damaged by the unnecessary drama and movement of new romance. She could see that I might want to help care for Shannon, but not why I would want to end my marriage to remain her lover. We drove up to Sweden one weekend, pottered around on the lake in the rowing boat. On a rare moment alone, she told me how much happier she thought I would be in the end if Hans and I just stayed together. There were many people invested in our relationship continuing – so many friends who liked us being a couple. Sometimes it was worth sticking with something, believing in the long durée. Lesbianism, or any other kind of sexual identity, really wasn't important in the longer perspective. When they'd tried it in the 1970s, it hadn't really worked. *You and Shannon*, she suggested, *will anyway be friends.*

I did not try to explain to her the way my pleasure in Shannon's body had bounced back after the stroke. Nor did I say how good it felt, even under the strange circumstances of her illness and newly limited vision, to have become her lover openly, and to find that role freed up for me by other people who were so actively her friends. Instead, I let my mother's category mistake sit a while. Many decades of different kinds of love might lead one to use the sliding scale between friendship and desire more freely. Back in the days when my mother read feminist arguments, important authors wrote about lesbianism as a form of companionate existence that might be chosen, a more platonic way of life offsetting corrupted forms of heterosexual desire. Twenty-five years earlier – the last time my mother ventured to give me a piece of direct advice, about not letting love take me to America – she'd already been good at blurring the categories. She'd advocated my home in Brighton with Imogen as offering a better life than my fledgling relationship with Hans. Her willingness to conflate love and friendship had ruffled me then, as it did now.

As a literary critic, one rarely argues for lovers becoming friends. But literary critics are well trained in diagnosing fictional friends as would-be lovers. In eighteenth-century studies this kind of argument sometimes lands on the example of Wollstonecraft, who spent two years living with the family of her best teenage friend, the talented illustrator Frances Blood. Theirs was *a friendship so fervent*, wrote Godwin of Wollstonecraft, *as for years to have constituted the ruling passion of her mind*. During those years Wollstonecraft and Blood laid out their plans for a life together. They opened a school in Newington Green, presenting it as a haven for female outcasts from married life. They persuaded Wollstonecraft's sister to leave her husband and join them. The project was designed to generate an income and secure an all-female household. But Blood got married, and her seafaring husband took her off to Lisbon in pursuit of a climate that would ease her bad health. Wollstonecraft followed the next year, to nurse Fanny after the birth of their child. After that, the school in Newington Green closed, without Mary there to keep it going.

Wollstonecraft's first novel, *Mary: A Fiction*, tells the story of a passionate friendship. The titular character Mary loves her friend Ann and supports her ardently and practically through illness and up until her death. Mary's feelings are dramatic and unorthodox, her disposition marked by a fierce passion that might be coded as masculine. At one point she's grilled by a group of women who suggest that a husband would be a better object than a friend for such levels of devotion. *Mary* as a novel responds to this challenge by being a treatise on passion as a principle to live by in all quarters of life, and by laying out a forthright rejection of marriage as a contract incompatible with intensely felt attachment. Like the texts that Wollstonecraft wrote later, this is a novel impatient with propriety.

Professionally I've always resisted the invitation to read a storyline like *Mary*'s as queer. I've preferred the line of argument that says one should read fiction written by and about women of the past not by shaking out the secret of lesbian desire, but by taking at face value what they tell us. In many cases, novels announce openly that friendship is the crux of emotional life. Emily Brontë compares friendship to a holly tree, love to the wild-rose briar, saying that one plant flowers in spring when everything inclines to bloom, while the other stays green and perversely bright in the depths of winter. Wollstonecraft clearly liked having sex with men, though she made plenty of claims for the enduring importance of women in her life. She wrote vividly of Fanny, her first daughter's namesake. She was also not coy about naming her pleasure in having a beautiful girl along for a coach ride. If she'd been into having sex with women, Wollstonecraft would probably have said so: her letters to Imlay make it clear that she had no problems representing other unconventional desires that she had.

Plenty of women in the past did have, and write about having, sex with each other. Anne Lister, the Yorkshire Tory, had a string of girlfriends from a young age and boasted in her diary of conquests that involved *feeling her all over pushing my finger up her etc.* Lister was not interested in being friends with these lovers. She was invested in being married to one of them. Mary Hamilton, star of Henry Fielding's earlier piece of sensational reportage, *The Female Husband*, was also quite clear about it being partnerships with women that she wanted. Her masculinity dazzling, Hamilton travelled around Somerset in the 1740s with a bag of dildos, marrying several women before one of them took her to court for a crime eventually defined as fraud. The women called up in court to witness Hamilton's treachery testified to their own ignorance in the matter of her sex, but one senses that they also knew what they wanted and could differentiate it very well from both love with men and friendship with women.

When reading novels, I usually have no trouble distinguishing stories about lovers from ones about friends. It never seems, for instance, that Ferrante's Lila and Lenù should find each other in bed; or that Jane Eyre and Helen should have. But I might be tempted to read my own life backwards, as queerer than it once seemed. To have fallen in love with Shannon in my late forties is inevitably to ask whether I have felt this kind of desire before, and whether friendship back then wasn't simply a code for a different kind of intimacy that I wanted to experience. Back in the days of life with Imogen, the boundary between the categories was perhaps less clear than I admitted as I sat in the bathroom, grinding my teeth over her casual affairs with men, listening greedily as she relayed the details of her sex life. I did read those gay novels. I did go swimming naked with a butch friend on that pebbly Brighton beach and imagine her swelling up with desire for me in some way that I could put my hands on. There was a time when Imogen went away for a month and said, as she was leaving, that I should *write to her every day*. In the depths of my crush on her, I took that literally and dropped pounds of loopy cursive letters into the mail-chute at the library where I worked, crouching between the shelves to write to her of silly things: the cat that had come in the window and slept on her bed, the man at the Marxist reading group who had kissed me. I found the letters under her bed months later, stuffed into a box where she kept floppy disks and nail polish, half of them unopened. There's no doubt she struggled with my avalanche of words – felt caught in that misplaced current of love.

My mother was wrong to imagine Shannon and I being just friends. But friendship was a term that I brandished oddly myself, in arguments with Hans after we broke up. On many walks around the harbour and the ramparts of the old city we tried to get our heads around the status of our new relationship. I said repeatedly that what I felt now was friendship. We'd negotiated everything together for so long, and I felt so deeply known to him. He was, and is, one of the only fixed points in my universe. But friendship, he argued, *was not the residue of love*. Broken down into its composite parts, one could not assume our marriage to have that other relation as its subset. If it had been love, why should that be downgraded now by my new romance? *Maybe what we call things is just a matter of time*, I argued. In conversations characterised sometimes by the memory of intimacy and sometimes by anger, we struggled over definitions.

Shannon grew stronger in good company in Philadelphia. *This is actually how I always wanted to live*, she said, her state of exuberance that autumn of 2019 puzzling and contagious. She was speaking not only of the particular relationships supporting her, but of friendship as a way of life: a reason to buy a house, take a job, refuse to have only one person listed on your hospital forms as your next of kin. I'd followed that same logic out of my childhood and across decades of wanting a life more porous to community than most married lives were. In modest ways, Hans and I had tried hard to build a life with friends. We'd shared cars and childcare and holidays and houses. In Copenhagen we'd eaten for years every Thursday night with a group of Danish neighbours who cooked big slabs of lasagne and pots of beans for each other. We'd had gangs of children trooping through our houses ever since Marie was old enough to invite them in. Hans had bought that cabin in Sweden with large gatherings in mind.

That group at Shannon's sickbed, and her celebration of it, reminded me of forms of feminism and hedonistic living that my parents had chosen as the best alternative to nuclear-family life. The people who cared for Shannon included her siblings, her kids, her colleagues. The circles they formed were enriched by kinship, even if not governed by family. This value they put on friendship was not queer by definition, nor was it only her queer friends who could provide this life. And yet, at least since the 1970s, friendship has been theorised better by critics of queer culture than straight. The term *friendship as a way of life* comes from an interview held in 1980 with the philosopher Michel Foucault, a few years before his death from AIDS. Foucault asks there: *How is it possible for men to be together? To live together, to share their time, their meals, their room, their leisure, their grief, their knowledge, their confidences? What is it to be naked among men, outside of institutional relation, family, profession and obligatory camaraderie?* He offers up homosexuality as a name for a universally desirable way of life, a language of community rather than a discrete form of sexual desire. The kinds of interaction he imagines for gay men becomes a model for connecting beyond the family and the institution. Precisely because it carries none of the weight of reproduction, marriage, inheritance and sex, friendship names that space of pleasurable and non-instrumental human interaction.

Foucault finds examples of this kind of connection in the classical past, when men occupied bathhouses and civic spaces. But he also imagines this as a future that homosexuality might portend. This is the utopian horizon *Another Country* helps bring into view. Friends in that novel connect in the spaces of New York City, in taxis and cinemas and squares, in bars and bedrooms, not at family dinner tables or workplaces or universities. The lust between Eric and Vivaldo, the relationship between Eric and Yves, the friendship of Rufus and Vivaldo, the fierce love between Ida and Vivaldo: all of these relationships are intimate tableaux rather than trajectories of development. Ida and Vivaldo won't marry, and Yves and Eric will almost certainly grow apart. And yet, like Foucault's account of friendship, *Another Country* invokes a non-professional community of friends as the basis for a well-lived life. The final scene, in which Yves lands in New York, blazes with hope for a new world in which there will be space for multiple kinds of connection. The Frenchman strides through the barriers of the airport *more high-hearted than he had ever been as a child, into that city which the people from heaven had made their home.* Baldwin's experience as a child preacher is put to good use. His hope extends to us, to the reading community that allows him to imagine dwelling in such a harmonious place. The novel's future is part of his optimism, hailing the ones who will love across professions and races and classes, without precedent or tradition, in freely chosen configurations that fiction has actively dreamed up for us.

Another Country belongs here, along with fictions like *Offshore* and *Monkey Grip*, to a small group of novels that have tried to make group relations rather than marriage their ethical horizon. A different account of the novel's literary treatment of friendship might stress, though, that friends and community haven't needed such horizons. Friends have always existed, real enough, despite the modest efforts of fiction writers at representing them. Jane Austen spent her last decades living in an ordinary house in Hampshire, which she shared with two female servants, her mother, her sister and Martha Lloyd, a family friend. In this household of six women there were no couples to speak of. But she never wrote a novel about a collection of single women living sustainably under one roof. The average sickbed in the nineteenth century probably looked more like Shannon's than a scene of conjugal devotion. Many of the constellations in which I was cared for as a child can be described as circles of friends rather than families. Arguably the novel's energy has been so fiercely directed towards the couple, or towards the utopian possibility of the friend, that it has not only ignored these realities, but has actively turned our fantasies away from their existence.

Those scenes make it hard for me to cede all that friendship to theorists and champions of queer community, or to credit them with imagining it as a way of life. I am often tempted to point out to friends and colleagues aligned with new queer formations that I grew up in a world that looked more like their utopia than the past they see themselves fighting against. But there's another part of me that accepts novels being to blame for this perception of previous decades and centuries having been populated by couples and nuclear families bent on romance and reproduction. Arguing that real life has not always been exactly like that – not for people mired in the historical reality of the nineteenth-century household or in the feminist collectives of the 1970s – doesn't help if the literature on which so many assumptions about the past are based suggests otherwise. It's true, novels don't have to show what we are really up to, but if they'd done a little more to document friendship, maybe they would have made the alliance between the gays and the socialists easier, and left queer theorists with less work to do.

Baldwin's version of love always has a political dimension. Both friendship and love appear in his writing as forces powerful enough to reconcile groups socially and racially divided. In *Another Country*, Vivaldo believes in individual connection as a corrective to the prejudice of the world he lives in, and in his relationships to Rufus and to Ida as reasons for optimism on this count. An essay he published in the *New Yorker* in 1962 calls for the individual as an agent in this progressive account of history: *Everything now is in our hands*, he writes.

> If we – and now I mean the relatively conscious whites and the relatively conscious blacks, who must, like lovers, insist on, or create, the consciousness of the others – do not falter in our duty now, we may be able, handful that we are, to end the racial nightmare, and achieve our country, and change the history of the world.

The self that is relatively conscious of racial injustice becomes someone who anticipates and drives social change, prompting the people he loves to follow suit.

And yet even within *Another Country* there is some doubt about whether love can do all this healing. *You'll be kissing a long time*, says Ida to Vivaldo of the relations between black and white America, *if you want to kiss away the hurt*. She sees racism as structural, a problem too endemic to society to be ameliorated by love, which has other qualities. Ida's view resonates with the one Arendt, that great friend of McCarthy, took as a philosopher. Arendt warned against love and friendship being used as a political anthem of any kind. *Love*, she argued, *by its very nature, is unworldly ... it is not only apolitical but antipolitical, perhaps the most powerful of all antipolitical human forces.* For this reason it cannot be harnessed on behalf of a group or a cause, cannot point you towards any community or any stranger, cannot fix a problem. On the high-profile platforms she occupied during the 1960s, Arendt insisted again and again, cigarette in hand, that one could not love the Jewish people, or women, or Germans.

In response to Baldwin's *New Yorker* essay, Arendt published a particularly severe response. *Dear Mr Baldwin*, she writes, *what frightened me in your essay was the gospel of love which you begin to preach at the end.* She goes on to reject Baldwin's emphasis on the fine qualities of black communities: *All the characteristics you stress in the Negro people: their beauty, their capacity for joy, their warmth, and their humanity, are well-known characteristics of all oppressed people. They grow out of suffering and they are the proudest possession of all pariahs.* With her own Jewishness in focus, Arendt argues that the characteristics one finds and responds to in a group are historically conditioned and subject to change. Any group one prefers for its powerlessness will be transformed when it comes to power. Social formations can be sponsored or contested, reconfigured or disputed, but not loved. Only individuals, seen for themselves alone, are the appropriate targets of affection.

Baldwin actually conceded to Arendt on this front, in print. He might have added that love, at least in *Another Country*, also helps undermine group affiliation. It's when Rufus and Vivaldo, and Eric and Vivaldo, are at their closest as friends that they are least visible as gay or straight, black or white. But if he had pressed this point, Arendt could have raised a different objection by stressing that real love of the here-and-now kind she prized still cannot be orientated towards a hypothetical future, a world that does not yet exist. Love can only connect you to those who are already around you. Arendt began making this argument in her PhD thesis on St Augustine, which takes issue with the idea of neighbourly love. Loving the stranger, she argues, makes no sense unless one is focused on a moment of redemption in which such generosity will bring reward. Properly practised in the private sphere, one's obligations when it comes to love can only be to what is given. This involves an opening-up to difference, a space-making, rather than a view of the future. In this iteration, friendship has nothing to do with political and religious strategies of kindness. *I love only my friends*, Arendt claimed. Her B and C and D are not political possibilities, not pledges to the future, but sites of absolute specificity.

By insisting that we locate friendship in the real world, Arendt draws very differently from Baldwin on non-romantic love as the key to making the future bearable. She approved of McCarthy's strategy in *The Group*, which was to describe her friends, rather than lavish them with kindness or hope. McCarthy may not approve of the women she brings to life, but the attention she gives individual characters is rare. She treats even their ugly, private desires with a kind of attention. It's the same attitude with which she attends to Arendt's ankles and her tastes in food, laying in the anchovy paste Hannah likes when she comes to stay, choosing birthday flowers for her. Rest assured, writes the poet W. H. Auden in 'For Friends Only', of your absolute originality; of the spare room that will be there only for you. *Come as you are*, writes

Hannah to Mary in this spirit: talk, play tennis, leave all generalities behind you.

I think of the many beds that were made for me when Shannon was sick, the places laid at tables. All of those small acts were part of Shannon's experience of being looked after in the way she recognised, and does well in return: the clothes bought for her, the bathroom rails installed, the equivalents of anchovy paste provided. I think of the letters in which people wrote to say in their own ways, *You have no double*. Of the possibility Shannon herself defends professionally, that descriptive fiction resonates with this version of friendship as the most generous grounds for engagement with actual difference. At the end of *Anna Karenina*, a room is being made up for a friend who is due to arrive. When Tolstoy diverts Levin from telling Kitty of his great revelation – that God exists only in the world around him, and in the action that world demands of him – it is to go off and act concretely and specifically on behalf of that friend.

One reason to linger here in Philadelphia in the late months of 2019, without getting back to the story of romance that I have been telling, would be to make friendship the form of this story's future. Fiction has not entirely failed friendship – it's here and there, filling a scene, defining an interaction, uplifting a plot from loss. Sometimes it even gets the last word. At the end of Toni Morrison's *Sula* – despite all evidence of betrayal – Nel is left missing her friend, Sula, more than the husband Sula stole from her. At the end of the *Neapolitan Quartet*, Lila has vanished and her friend Lenù is left writing about her. One could argue that friendship is better represented in these moments than the stuff of everyday family life, which remains anathema to plot and harder to display without smugness. But the novel in which friendship keeps going, solid and sustainable, grounded in small acts of kindness and honesty, is hard to find. If there are many days when reality reveals that to be possible, it's not in the novel's DNA to capture it.

Just as I once wanted us to stay in that first erotic spring, now I am tempted to leave us sitting around a year later, dreaming of capacious farmhouses and trips we will take north – of the more collective formations in which we might live. If I could choose, it would be like that. Not a future of the temporal kind at all, but a place of many spare rooms; many relations other than the biological and professional ones that tug at us again; many trips to see friends across the country on trains. I did not much like Sarah Orne Jewett's *Country of the Pointed Firs* when I first read it for graduate school, but I like it now: small, rural houses connected by visits between women; family supplanted by something more accidental and open to encounter. It makes me think of the Maine in which Hardwick ultimately did arrive: her barn complete, her friends around her, Harriet coming to visit, Lowell again her friend – a scene that *Sleepless Nights* does not capture, but out of which it finally arose. It might be here that the documentary element of this story peels off from the formal ones I have been exploring, about what it means to have lived a life so closely intertwined with the stories told in novels. For many who have done so, that page of acknowledgements, written last, is the supplement to every plot.

Chapter Nine

LOVE OF THE TEACHER

Yet it was work we turned to that autumn, and to Rohan and
Marie in Copenhagen. Shannon was still on sick leave, but
my job was firmly in Copenhagen, where I ran an institute at
Denmark's oldest university, teaching 'Love and the Novel'
in a new context. We agreed that Shannon would come for
a few months, and she arrived for the New Year's party that
friends threw to welcome 2020. It was a different and happier threshold from the last one I'd crossed, alone with my
thoughts on *Pride and Prejudice* in the Swedish forest, but
it was not the perfect constellation. Hans and I remained
caught up in both bad-tempered altercations and old rituals.
Shannon and Marie were meeting for the first time, and
Rohan did not seem much ready for a new version of family
life. For most people in the world, work remains less nego-
tiable than love, while often being the hardest element of life
to reconcile with the values of independence and individual-
ity that the novel has encouraged us to uphold.

The year since Shannon's arrival, in which the global pandemic has forced us into a ceaseless crush of familiarity, and
changed dramatically the nature of our jobs, has trumped
many of the fears I had about being too much in the thrall

of love. In the small space we have shared there is only one round table. Since March 2020 it has stayed crowded with bits of our lives. The US absentee voters' ballot has come and gone in its special envelope. Shannon's laptop, streaming discussions of racial justice in the American University, has competed almost daily with mine, reporting news of sexual harassment and reduced budgets in the Danish one. Random pieces of Rohan's birthday Lego have gathered in the fruit bowl; an edible pumpkin has been hollowed out for Halloween; candles put up in a spirit of hapless concession to ritual that would have had Laura Ingalls Wilder laying down her pen in satisfaction. We've sat around this table for Skype drinks, for meals with Rohan and Marie, for virtual classes and meetings at all times of the night and day.

As the virus came to Denmark in March 2020, I was teaching that 'Love and the Novel' course. We'd planned for Shannon to make some guest appearances – forays into teaching that would allow her to experiment with teaching, while being unable to read print as she once had. Shannon had just given a lecture on de Beauvoir when the university shut down. Friends who had been visiting from New York flew home in haste, and we were left to figure out how to bring the students to life on the screen; how to lead, under these new conditions, conversations about Thomas Hardy and D. H. Lawrence; to ask how novels might guide us in a world from which all proper forms of human plot seem drained suddenly away. To think about novels in 2020 was to confront all the ways in which fiction cannot represent the unexpected, cannot directly fix the harms of plague or war, cannot connect us to the people we care most about. And yet to be left with language to work with, with only the virtual classroom, was not quite to be left with nothing.

It is here, as I find myself curving back to that question I borrowed from Hardwick – of what a life told in books might look like – that I face in the last instance my life as a student and a teacher in service to fiction. At this table, work is hard to ignore. It's a force more determinate of life than it is of fictional plots. There's no doubt the novel arises out of, and gives rise to, forms of work that are often absent from our discussions of fiction. The classroom, for instance, is missing from Foucault's list of ideal spaces of friendly association. Foucault excludes it from this list because it belongs to another list he keeps, of spaces where power is negatively exercised by institutions and internalised by those who populate them. I do not blame him for leaving that space out of his account of friendship. A classroom, in the end, is not a horizontal or a freely defined society. It is dominated by a teacher, complicated for that reason as a setting in which to locate love. But it is also a space akin on this count, in its inequality, to the fictional worlds in which one mind is constitutionally more equal and more beloved than others.

I felt that most acutely when I was a student during another moment of historical crisis nearly twenty years ago. In 2001 Hans and I were living in Princeton in one of those little huts rented by the university to graduate students. On 11 September I was up early taking notes on *Lolita* for my favourite seminar, scheduled to be held that afternoon, a class that was itself about novels and their relation to reality. Our teacher's thesis was that novels that cleaved most closely to real objects and surfaces often failed as narrative. I was considering this that morning in relation to vegetable matter: the magnolia flowers that floated in the branches of the tree beside our porch, the tended institutional lawns spread out like crops to be juiced and consumed. In *Lolita*, Humbert Humbert is disappointed by American greenery, even though he's so drunk on everything else in the new world. As I read and underlined Vladimir Nabokov's sentences in preparation for class, the men who maintained the grounds were working above me, taking handfuls of autumn leaves down from the gutters, their air-machines emitting a faint smell of metal and their radio sending music tinkling across the roof. It was their shouting to each other about planes flying into buildings that made me put down *Lolita* and go onto the porch to find out what was happening.

After that, Hans and I stood in our pyjamas in the kitchen, listening to a radio station in Newark reporting about a hijacked plane being still up in the air. We made coffee and stared up at the sky through the branches of the tree. The workers drove away in their university truck, leaving canvas bags of leaves half stuffed beside our porch, an aluminium ladder propped against the house. Hans went, like the workers, to watch television somewhere else, leaving me to dress. I lingered in the house then, toying with the idea I could just keep reading *Lolita*. Mourning the loss of the class that was cancelled, I longed for my teacher, who was small with short, grey hair and a scowl that came easily, when all her other gestures were economical. She had trained us to think about single sentences, often letting the first line of a novel guide our whole discussion. Why does the author put the colon there? Why does he imagine the road as wet?

She'd gather answers democratically before rearranging them in importance, using what we'd said to show something that had probably been in her mind all along. Her classes taught me that the combination of weather and tile in a sentence could produce a special kind of verisimilitude not there in descriptions of architectural detail alone. She never spoke about real events, not even after so many died in Manhattan. But her class on the novel suggested that everything you needed to know was on the page and, if you read well enough, you could work it out. I was riveted. What she said about objects related closely to the desire that often beset me to cram her scarf into my mouth and eat it whole. How could someone so determined to deflect attention away from herself be so desirable?

Later that autumn I went into a jewellery shop in the West Village and bought myself a watch on display in the window, plain silver with a tight mesh band that slid back and forth across the inside of my arm. I was conscious of it there on my wrist at a party thrown that evening by an important male professor in New York. It was the kind of party that's become hard to picture now, people sitting along the walls in the hallway and stepping over each other's legs, kissing strangers. Someone offered me coke in a bathroom tucked away at the back of the apartment. I shook my head, looking at the time to see whether we could still catch the last NJ transit train home. In the class on novels, which resumed a few weeks after 11 September, I realised that my new watch matched absolutely the one my teacher wore. It went into my bag, an object burning with proof of desire.

I have worn that watch on most teaching days since, taking

it off and putting it on the desk in front of me when class starts. In 2020 it joined the jumble of things on the crowded table, ticking away the quarter-hours into which a discussion of a novel can be sliced, even on Zoom. It reminds me of the love it is possible to feel towards someone with the power to suggest ideas you couldn't reach alone. Reading Jane Austen or James Joyce or Henry James can feel like that to me, too. I know, as many have argued, that there's a case to be made for novels as vehicles of democracy, and generosity, and for the engagement they promote with different points of view. But if we imagine them only as models for these horizontal ways of living, we miss something of the artist, sitting, as Joyce describes, *within or behind or beyond or above his handiwork, invisible, refined out of existence, indifferent, paring his fingernails.* In this construction, novels are spectacles of control, arguments for an inequality that classrooms and fiction can share as structures. My watch is a reminder of the pleasure that comes from becoming the person in the sway of another.

One of fiction's most famous teachers, Lucy Snowe, is the narrator of Charlotte Brontë's *Villette*. Lucy is a teacher in a small Flemish Catholic boarding school, employed to teach English to girls with the kinds of privilege and visibility she's never had. Her story is more difficult and less well known than Jane Eyre's. *Villette* is a romance, but it is better described as the story of a woman making her career abroad – a novel that puts Lucy's work at the centre of her relation to the world rather than suggesting marriage is her only option. Lucy differs from Jane, who also works for some time in a charity school, but is always bent in her telling of this story towards her union with Rochester and her future vocation as his wife. In neither case is working as a teacher presented as easy. Lucy is not like Madame Beck, her employer, the busybody director of the school who runs things with a firm hand and a prurient gaze; or like M. Paul Emanuel, the charismatic literature professor basking in the loving gaze of his students with his beret, his little glasses, arms in his loose blouse, hands trailing cigar smoke. He tutors Lucy in maths, pouring his knowledge almost jauntily into her lap, then pouting in public when he thinks she has no gift for him on his name-day; he takes his students to breakfast in the countryside and reads them stories in the evening. For Lucy, on the other hand, the classroom is a terrifying place, one that plays a part in the psychological breakdown she experiences in the course of the novel.

When asked about teaching, Lucy describes it as a job, something she does to support herself. *Do you like it?* probes her friend and young rival, Polly. *Not always. And why do you go on with it? Chiefly,* answers Lucy with characteristic candour, *for the sake of the money I get ... and for the comfort of mind it gives me to think that while I can work for myself, I am spared the pain of being a burden to anybody.* Despite her frank presentation of teaching as labour, it's in the role of teacher that she delivers *Villette*'s story. *What are you,* her flighty student Ginerva pesters: *are you anybody? I am,* replies Lucy, *a school-teacher.* That designation suffices in making her *known where she should be known,* trumping other questions of pedigree and appearance and social position. Describing herself this way, Lucy controls a narrative where she sees and engineers the encounters between characters, but remains figuratively and sometimes literally off to the side of the story she tells.

Many of the authors I have taught, on 'Love and the Novel', might also have replied in this spirit about their professional lives, answering that question of what they *really were* by detailing their work as teachers of literature. Charlotte Brontë was herself this kind of teacher for a while, as were Elizabeth Hardwick, Vladimir Nabokov, Penelope Fitzgerald, Toni Morrison, Ali Smith. All of them have taught, written in the margins of books they must explain the next day, directed the attention of their students away from their selves and towards a scenario unfolding on the page. Fitzgerald, author of *Offshore*, spent twenty-six years of her life teaching English in privileged North London schools, always describing this as work she struggled with. Ex-students remember her as scruffy and bad-tempered. She was not obviously beloved or besotted. But those portraits of Martha and Tilda in *Offshore*, so sensitively drawn as children, suggest Fitzgerald knew her subjects well. Despite what she said about not liking her teaching, she kept doing it as her acclaim and income as a novelist grew. The fictional and historical worlds of her novels, most of which are populated with children portrayed by a caring and attentive narrator, have the same feeling as the classroom in the control of someone good – someone with the authority to read the students, anticipate the dynamics, choreograph the outcome.

We hear so often these days of institutional power being abused that it has become almost impossible to advocate for its beauty, its erotic potential. As a teacher learning my trade in America, I had to sit in mandatory workshops cautioning me not to take students home, to buy them drinks, to talk to them about my life. At one weekend event for a group of the new faculty at the University of Michigan, I watched an academic dean spell out the implications of such transgression, drawing out from a cardboard box examples of love letters, cassette tapes, photographs that incriminated those who had crossed the line. *If you have that song in your heart,* he said, *don't write it down; for God's sake,* if it must be, *let your students be desired in silence.* We nodded and took notes. Then, from the back of the room, came the question: *What about love?* It was a male professor of physics, newly arrived from Italy, and all of us turned to him in unison, imagining with concern his students falling for a teacher from the old world who did not know the righteous rules of this new one.

But if we do not engage with love as something solicited, sometimes, by power, we risk being unable to explain at least part of what keeps us coming back to novels as worlds over which one person holds a quiet and powerful sway. D. A. Miller celebrates Austen's narrator as a model of style, claiming her version of personhood as one he will spend his life as a critic trying to emulate, summing up the temptation of many to worship at her feet. Others feel this way about Joyce and his nail-paring narrator, or Henry James and his inimitable sentences, the intelligence and beauty of his prose. Rightly or wrongly, readers have experienced these feelings about authors from the very beginning of the novel's history, even as they were also being taught by fiction to challenge what they knew, to reassess what they felt and to be completely obedient to no one.

From their first issue, novels have also provided stories that endorsed the idea of love being directed towards someone with more power than you. Rousseau's *Julie; or, the New Eloise* – that explosive hit of the 1760s – explores in microscopic detail the noble Julie's love for her tutor. Written just a few decades after *Pamela*, *Julie* confirmed readers' hunger for stories in which lovers are not equal. Readers of fiction were primed early to delight in Elizabeth Bennet finding her mate in the older and richer Darcy; in the younger Emma being corrected by the self-righteous Knightley; in homeless Jane taking Rochester as her surly senior; in Carol taking the sexually naïve Therese on the road; in Ali Smith's awkward teenager, Magnus, being sexually initiated in *The Accidental* by a mysterious older woman. Not *Lolita*, maybe: there's got to be a limit. But right up to that point, and sometimes even past it, we have been attuned by novel-reading to the guilty pleasure of being in the hands of someone better, to the possibility that this might be the most desirable thing of all.

It's deep in the form of fiction: the possibility that one person can initiate another into passion. Novel-reading would never have become as popular as it's been for the last 300 years if it did not hail us all as people who can follow authorial directive on this front, lead our bodies to respond to the suggestions of someone we don't actually know. *On Earth We're Briefly Gorgeous*, a novel validating sexual submission as a kind of joy, is being taught right now to students who can hardly believe their luck at being assigned a book that explains the pleasure of being fucked by someone too powerful to let you return the favour. They are discussing the erotics of inequality while revelling in Ocean Vuong's skill as a writer, his mastery in describing one lover's crucifix held in the mouth of the other as he is being penetrated. He is writing with such skill about surrender in the context of race and class in America that readers feel accommodated by that story even as they slip into Vuong's own power, become students who would let him do anything he asked, take their minds anywhere he wanted.

The classroom and the novel are not simple analogues of each other. Yet they introduce in comparable ways the pleasures of someone else knowing more, even about your own desires, and of having this pleasure become legitimate. I have never wanted to be in the hands of a teacher the way I wanted to be taught by the professor who had me wearing her watch and drilling down into the sentences on the page for answers to the questions she asked. But I have been in the arms of my literary elders often enough to know it can feel good to experience power in this way. One of them, who was himself obsessed with the figure of the older teacher, first taught me Rousseau. Inspired by feelings he got while being beaten as a child, Rousseau pursued fantasies of lying *at the feet of an imperious mistress, obeying her commands, asking her forgiveness*. For the better part of his teens, he lived with Madame de Warens, the older woman described with adoration in *The Confessions*, becoming her lover after years of being her student. He went on to write books arguing that humans were badly served in their morality by society, *born free but everywhere in chains*. We are confined by social conventions, he argued, as unfortunately as saplings in the middle of a highway. He saw the lover as infinitely educable, believed in the student's innate capacity to connect with the world erotically, a teenager capable in this one arena of desire of proper entanglement with other people.

Hannah Arendt, advocate of friendship as the highest form of love between those different and equal, also knew about this dynamic of inequality. In her first year at Marburg University she began an affair with the university's most popular and well-respected philosophy lecturer, Martin Heidegger. She was eighteen when she became his lover. She looks good in pictures from that time, shoes buckled, stockings white under her simple dress, hair curling around her neck. She doesn't look like someone who would sign up for any journey by accident. But Heidegger looks good, too. He was thirty-five, and married with two small sons, when Hannah appeared in his class. He never considered making their affair public or leaving his wife, and when things became difficult he all but forced Hannah to leave town. Years later, when her books were as famous as his, Heidegger was churlishly reluctant to read them, suggesting he'd find her English hard.

This relationship, impossible to celebrate as a relation between equals, is more galling in its facts than the fictional relationship between Lucy Snowe and M. Paul. Yet we cannot speak honestly of the classroom or the novel as models for love without recognising its appeal. Under the right circumstances, I would have taken all the parts of her body that my teacher had offered. I would have gone down on my knees anywhere she wanted. Not just because she was a woman so fine-looking and smart, but because she was a person far out ahead of me in her acquisition of knowledge. Even now I like to think of Hannah unhooking Martin's cufflinks, relics from the nineteenth century, his shirts ironed by a poor woman who comes in to help his wife. He sits back and watches her lift her dress. Hannah wears the well-cut clothes of someone ready to travel into twentieth-century America, but for a while there's nothing she'd rather do than take them off for Martin. This scene is hotter than anything between fellow students could ever be. At twenty-three, the pleasure I got in Hans's grown-up ways was the most extreme I'd ever known. He was only a few years ahead of me, but all the things that made him older – the Proust and the pipes, the tweed jackets, the knowledge of European history and the back streets of Tanzania – were the things I wanted most.

Ten years into our relationship, once things had evened out in our marriage, I helped out on a friend's course at the University of British Columbia, taking over a class during her sickness. That week she'd assigned Carol Ann Duffy's poem 'Little Red Cap'. The poem is a rewriting of 'Little Red Riding Hood' and a description of Duffy's life as a student who begins her career at sixteen by sleeping with an older poet, a man famous enough to be giving a reading in her small British home town. The poem describes him standing in a clearing, reading his verse, wolf-like in his wine-stained appeal:

> *In the interval, I made quite sure he spotted me*
> *Sweet sixteen, never been, babe, waif, and bought me a*
> *drink.*

In Duffy's account, she goes to the lair of the wolf, in thrall to his books, trusting his capacity to get her out of that small town. She stays ten years, the poem says, reading her fill and finding the strength to kill the wolf, which is when she discovers his stomach filled with her grandmother's bones.

The students I taught that day in Vancouver weren't impressed with 'Little Red Cap'. They were keen to moralise about the older man and the younger girl. *She was only sixteen. It was illegal*, they insisted. He should have been arrested. *It was exploitation. She should have had other ways to get an education*. I remember that class because I was incredibly tired. Hans was already away teaching in Denmark, and I was alone with Marie. I'd been bleeding that night from what I feared would become a miscarriage. I went on working because the day seemed unbearably grim otherwise. We hadn't meant for me to be pregnant, but it would have been nice to have another child, to have embraced the kind of settled life that would make that something to celebrate. I didn't care much about the Duffy poem, but I had no patience with the students' pious insistence that only love between equals was proper. *Let me teach you some things about actual love*, I wanted to say.

That day, in my mood of incipient loss and parental responsibility, I would myself have liked a teacher who knew how to profess; to rescue me from the responsibility of being the only adult in the classroom; to take me to the edge of town; to skew that situation of equality in which Hans and I had found ourselves in our thirties. To hell with all that, I wanted to say through my fatigue: look where it has brought us, all this sharing of power and income and free time. All this taking turns to wash the clothes and pay the bills; all the family planning gone wrong and the insistence on doing it fairly and being true to each other's needs, when in fact no one is really getting to do what they want, which is just sit still and read. Is this really where desire lies? Don't you ever simply want someone who will tell you how to do it? To whom you will open up all the spaces in your body? Or someone to wash the clothes and care for the children while you sit with your book? I didn't say any of that. But I viewed the young Canadians wearily, their waves of decency washing away the eros of the poem. If you want to boycott all the loves that have emerged from the desire to be in the hands of someone else, I thought, you've got your work cut out for you.

In theory, the sheer and explicit power of a mentor like Heidegger does not interest me. I do not endorse the old habits of seduction and exploitation. But the pleasure I have felt as the student led away from the rest of the class, singled out for love, is not unlike the way it can feel to me to open a novel and have a narrator start telling me exactly what I need to know. The pleasure of being the reader can resemble the pleasure of being the chosen one, permitted to drink straight from the source, to stay in the gallery after hours, freed from having to ask or to compete, or even pretend you know as much. Of having Shannon to myself when the laptop screen closes on her American students and we are left to ourselves – me listening to her talk about all the things she knows best against the background noise of the Danish bells pealing into the night.

I am shackling them together, the novel and the classroom, as spaces in which love and power can help, under the right circumstances, to make sense of each other. And yet from that corollary arises my related sense that the best teachers, like the best narrators, are those that refuse a certain kind of advantage and know how to redistribute power. In the days when we lived together, Imogen gave me a book of essays by the philosopher Gillian Rose. Those essays are deeply personal, yet in the best of them of them Rose says little about herself. Instead she tells the stories of people she has known: an older friend dying of cancer, a friend with AIDS, an Eastern European aristocrat whose property is restored to him long after it was taken in the war. She presents these friends as teachers to whom she is indebted for her insight that it can be best to dwell *in the fray*. Life's real achievement, Rose insists, is to fade into the world and become part of it. *I aspire*, she writes, *to Miss Marple's persona: to be exactly as I am, decrepit nature, yet supernature in one, equally alert on the damp ground and in the turbulent air*. Her own death looms in those essays as something that will deprive her tragically of the invisibility that comes naturally with old age. Rose's argument flips the normal logic of mortality around. The luxury of having time to become part of the crowd, the senior who is not seen, teacher rather than first-person protagonist.

In *Villette*, Lucy knows how to live and teach and narrate from that midst. She is not old, but she is small and physically almost impossible to pin down. As a real person, she stays beyond our grasp, hard to catch in action. To her students, she gives almost nothing away, no emotion or preference. She refrains from embracing them, conducts lessons lacking the smooth authority of the other teachers at the school. And yet the almost recessive relation she has to her own tale illuminates that mystery of what makes her a good teacher, observant of the world of which she remains a part. Brontë wrote *Villette* under conditions that must have made it hard to relish that position. All three of her siblings died the year of its composition. As teaching keeps Lucy going – accepting of her world as it is, resistant to the solace of Catholicism – one imagines writing this novel as a thing Brontë worked at.

Lucy's redemption arrives in the form of love from M. Paul Emanuel, her older teacher. The two find each other slowly, across the barrier of age and culture, impeded by their individual, shadowy histories of loss. The climax of their romance comes when M. Paul presents Lucy with a room. It's a place he's arranged for her painstakingly in his last days in Europe before taking a long voyage that will postpone their marriage indefinitely. As part of his preparations for departure, he's rented Lucy a house with space to teach in, and has printed business cards for the school she is to start. Perhaps he dominates too fully the scenario. Yet he bequeaths Lucy her own power generously, his parting gift to her, declaring that he loves her before bowing out from the last chapter of the novel.

There is something about the room M. Paul gives to Lucy, recognising her ability to fill it on her own terms, which moves me closer to tears than almost any romantic ending. I almost never cry over novels, but I have cried over this one. Lucy's classroom reminds me of that space that Arendt celebrates as the one worldly lovers and friends give to each other – the one McCarthy exercises in laying in just the right things for her visits. The bed made at the end of *Anna Karenina*. The scene also reveals M. Paul as a teacher who knows how to make way for others. The unrealised marriage becomes a model for people ceding ground to each other. At its culmination, *Villette* promises a geography, not a future, that can accommodate happiness and difference. That classroom, and not the family scene at Christmas, is where Brontë invests her hope.

If only, we might say, Martin had been more inclined to read Hannah's books, or Duffy's wolf-poet to give her a library of her own. But these writers have both emphasised the importance of their real-life teachers in making their careers. Duffy claims she and the poet stayed friends. Heidegger's letters to Arendt are full of enormous devotion and encouragement. He testifies there to the quality of their connection as well as to his support of her future as a philosopher. As she became a famous freethinker, a critic of totalitarianism, an advocate of worldly engagement, Arendt stayed true to Heidegger in some way. She returned to him regularly over the next fifty years, naming her intellectual debt, paying her dues, reviving affection over drinks in hotels. From America, she defended him against charges of anti-Semitism and denied evidence of his alliance with the National Socialists. She read his new books knowing that he would not read hers, confiding in letters to McCarthy that he had been the great love of her life.

Again, this is not a defence. I am invested in Lucy Snowe, not Martin. I am invested in being in the fray. In getting old enough for that. In being the teacher and the writer good enough to fade away, a thing that hasn't always been easy for me to do. It's a lesson that goes against others I have taken to heart, as a girl trying to be bigger and more outspoken, a foreigner making myself heard at all, a lover saying, *This is what I want.* But I know, as a teacher, that the power to dictate matters less than the ability to retreat and leave the stage, and that this too belongs to the logic of narrative control.

In those days of being besotted with my own teacher, the part of the Arendt and Heidegger story that troubled me was the part about Elfriede, Heidegger's wife. She is known for giving Heidegger the famous *Hütte* in the mountains where he went to write his philosophy, but she's gone down badly in history. Of the two, she was the one who believed definitively that Germany needed cleansing of its *Jewish-Marxist influence.* Elfriede's anti-Semitism clearly had a personal side to it. Once Heidegger told her about his affair with Arendt, she made herself into a threshold between them. She didn't entirely sanction Arendt's visits, but she controlled them. Later in life, when the three of them had learned to tolerate each other, Elfriede referred to Hannah as her friend. But her prejudices came through when she wrote asking for help in the final years: Hannah was a Jew and must know about money. Could she help dispose profitably of Martin's manuscripts?

I read about Elfriede in the fake oldness of the Firestone Library at Princeton. I was meant to be reading Heidegger's *Being and Time*, but I wanted to know if he was as bad personally as rumour had it. I drifted, as one did back then, between shelves and books, down into the stacks, into the margins where Elfriede was mentioned. I learned that for a while during the 1930s her belief in National Socialism made her a beloved teacher of teenage girls. This kept me reading because I connected her story by this thread to that of another teacher I knew, from Muriel Spark's *The Prime of Miss Jean Brodie*. Jean Brodie uses her charms in the classroom that same decade as Elfriede was teaching. *The Prime of Miss Jean Brodie*, which I bought at Gay's the Word bookshop along with *Maurice* and *The Swimming Pool Library* from wages earned at the supermarket, follows a whole group of girls who become the *crème de la crème* of an Edinburgh school, singled out by their teacher for attention and after-hours instruction. She invites them to tea and takes them to parts of the old city they would never go to alone. With textbooks propped open on their desks as cover against sudden visits from the headmistress, they tune in with various degrees of enthusiasm and infatuation to stories of Miss Brodie's trips to Europe and her outlandish love affairs. Jean Brodie takes the cult of personality to extremes. She is M. Paul Emanuel with his blouses and cigars – only worse, because these are years in which there are so many opportunities to identify with uniforms and the wrong sort of power.

Jean Brodie finds Hitler *rather naughty*, but during his reign she is *quite sure the new regime would save the world*. Spark presents her with irony, acknowledging the cult teacher to be terrible, unprofessional, politically inappropriate. But her style of spinsterhood is also brave and it offsets her misappropriation of power, revealing her to be sexually awake in ways that justified Spark's place on the shelves of Gay's the Word. And here, too, part of the ambiguity lies in the victory of the student over the teacher. Jean Brodie's star student, Sandy, triumphs as the implied author of Spark's novel. Like Mary-Alice, the author of *Asymmetry*, she ends up representing her teacher, writing about the scenes in which the undeniable charm of the mentor is outgrown by the student who sees through it, and whose own novel succeeds by being more generous towards others than the lessons in which it originated. The last slim section of *Asymmetry* tests our view of Ezra as he is brought down to size by his appearance on a radio show, the great novelist diminished by his miserly answers to a series of banal questions. *Asymmetry* overall cranks open the architecture of the kind of self-regarding American novel that Ezra writes, opening the gates wide to the character of Amar Jaafari, an Iraqi-American man, while leaving space for us to see Ezra himself as having once been Mary-Alice's teacher.

Elfriede Heidegger's teacherly skills are not clearly recorded, although her husband suggests in various letters that they were excellent. Some pieces she wrote in defence of National Socialism can still be read online. In them, she states quite reasonably that all women should have access to proper and equal education. It is in the interests of the state for girls to be well read and informed. They might not be men, but they are mothers of men and part of the national collective in their own right. Elfriede went further than Jean Brodie in seizing this chance to teach women a love of art and literature as well as a love of military power. She oversaw her students as they became ditch-diggers for the state later in the war. She may even have instructed them well in the use of a spade. Maybe the girls got strong and had time to read in the afternoons. But Elfriede's anti-Semitism was brazen. That night in the library, the evidence of this lay for me in the fact that she had left no one to write about her, certainly not the way Arendt did of Heidegger. And in the fact that her shelves were bare of novels. *She reads only the most terrible things*, writes Arendt to McCarthy, letting this be enough to indict Elfriede for having failed to understand all sides of the story.

For in the end, neither novels nor teachers are meant to attract our unconditional love, our support for everyone or anything they represent. One virtue of learning from fiction rather than fact is that it weans us off uncritical judgement. Reading fiction may be a discipline in the context of the classroom, but it is also about seeing through authority. It has been this for as long as people have placed novels on the side of the Enlightenment against religion, of the Romantic revolutionaries against convention, on the side of women with the power to choose their own loves and remake the moral codes that they are told to follow. Novels cannot be used easily to rally students to any one set of opinions, and the best of them are excluded from the dictator's shelf. Those who love them rarely end up doing anything they say, except perhaps observing well, and caring about a reality from which they seem constitutionally to differ.

And so Shannon and I end up as teachers, fading into the fray. It's not a very romantic plot, but it's the one Hardwick might have followed when she considered the currents on which she coasted through most of the twentieth century. She too kept teaching literature and writing about it, making books her work, building up that guild of which we are still minor members. More romantically, living with Shannon reminds me daily of having had teachers who were stylish and self-effacing enough to get me to have, and to reconsider, my own thoughts. Life with a person so skilled at thinking about and clearing space for other people is dazzlingly good. It has aspects of a life I once dreamed of leading in the company of Austen's narrator, or of that teacher long ago. Shannon, who for the purposes of this story might be the character who admits only *I am a teacher*, knows how to read the room, anticipate the sway of feeling, bring everyone into the story. Being with her makes me aware of quiet adulation as one of the many kinds of love that is possible.

Great fictions are invitations to live in worlds already unfolded, already seen, imagined, by a mind many steps ahead of the reader. This is as much a part of their pleasure as the promotion of the individual, or the recognition of others. Reading the right novel can involve trusting oneself to someone so good at being human – so skilled at perceiving what that might be – that you can only hope to follow along behind them for a while. Even an author who turns out in real life to be utterly fallible can bequeath to the reader a world that contradicts, in its prefabricated beauty, the way real thinking and action work. In novel worlds, there are no pandemics and accidents and strokes, because even when these things are represented, they are events conceived of for us by someone else.

This is not to negate the ways that reading a novel involves feeling seen in one's own particularity. The reader is the friend whose bed has been made; for whom there is a space in the world as it is, because of the world made bigger by fiction. It is an extraordinary feature of the novel that a story planned and executed – like a class perfectly taught, or a house beautifully built – can be both an island birthed and designed, and a place that invites you in your particularity to enter. A novel world is both entirely there and open to change, both fixed and generous to interpretation. Austen, as I have sometimes argued in my life as a critic, gives us the marriage and the wedding, all the parts already in place, a happy ending foreseen from the outset. Yet she knows entirely that real life is full of fallen women; couples tired of each other's company; spinsters bound in friendship; second sons for whom there is no estate to populate; survivors of tragedy who live to tell their tales; and even, I like to think, women who live together. It's between that messiness of an uncertain reality and the beauty of a hypothesis, between the world's contingencies and the already-thereness of its stories, that a reader must wend her way.

ON ENDINGS

The Price of Salt, that novel I had on my lap the first time I flew to meet Shannon, did not originally have a happy ending. Highsmith had to be persuaded by her editor to bring it to that unlikely point of closure where Therese and Carol find each other again, and Carol invites Therese to move in with her. The pages uplifting me that night on the runway as I was waiting for my own story to begin were an afterthought, a revision. Even as I was stuck there, I recognised them as a poor fix for a tale that should more realistically have ended in grief or heartache, or died down into the humdrum reality of childcare and work. Yet Highsmith – famously curmudgeonly about human relations, and known in the end for her love of snails and isolation – allows Therese and Carol to find each other in fiction. *Happiness is as good an ending as any other*, she seems to say with a shrug. *Let's give them happiness*.

Forty years earlier, E. M. Forster struggled with the similar problem of how to end *Maurice*, a novel he had no plans to publish. A love story focused on two men, *Maurice* was written in the 1910s as the persecution of homosexuals in England was in full swing, and was only published posthumously in 1971. At the end of the novel, Oxford-educated

Maurice renounces his social position to be with Alec Scudder, a worker on his friend's estate. To get them firmly into each other's arms, Forster had to remove them almost entirely from Edwardian society. In one ending he wrote, they turn up living happily together as woodcutters. Looking back on that piece of creative engineering, Forster writes: *A happy ending was imperative. I shouldn't have bothered to write otherwise. I was determined that in fiction anyway two men should fall in love and remain in it for the ever and ever that fiction allows, and in this sense Maurice and Alec still roam the greenwood.*

It's tempting to insist that these endings are artificial because it was so difficult for gay couples to live openly together for most of the twentieth century. And yet Forster wrote *Maurice* after a visit to his friend Edward Carpenter, who spent the second half of his long life living with George Merrill, the son of an engine builder. Forster had an example of domestic felicity more concrete than that of many authors around him, who sent their straight characters off more casually to set up house in the greenwood. *Reader, I married him*, says Jane Eyre, announcing her long-awaited union with Rochester with a famous lack of enthusiasm. Of Emma's marriage to Knightley, Austen can only bring herself to announce primly that *the wishes, the hopes, the confidence, the predictions of the small band of true lovers who witnessed the ceremony, were fully answered in the perfect happiness of the union.* Comparatively speaking, the last scenes of *Maurice* and *The Price of Salt* feel quite promising.

Perhaps it's not an ending's particular features that make it artificial, but the fact that it must be there at all. Most real lives are so long and so persistent that there is room enough in them for many things to change. Literary lives would look different if characters had the chance most of us really do get: to carry on past our prime, reel from one disaster to the next, watch our friends grow older, estrange our children and re-find them, remake our families. A novel that captured loving from all those angles would be unfathomably complex. But it's not up to novelists to represent everything. In stories, the line has to get drawn somewhere.

In my own life, though, sometimes when I am drifting into sleep, the curl of Shannon's back within reach, Rohan asleep close by, this does feel like happiness. The scenes I witness, like the ones playing inside my head, are often golden. Rohan swims in the Copenhagen harbour now, jumping wide into the water like a fish, surfacing, swimming, diving in again. Shannon and I sometimes follow him in, then lie on the pontoon and talk with him about things he likes: burgers, Teslas, books. If I recall the events that have happened in the last years, the plot seems like a bad one: Shannon nearly dying, a plague coming, rage and breakage. In the past the prospect of the water rising, a missed plane or a child's hurt feelings was enough to make me worry. Now all those things, and worse, have happened and I am still here telling tales in the light of a long Nordic evening.

Apart from the love of a good sentence, novels have given me a way of being lightly on the Earth, anticipating the greenwood as a place to read, as well as to make love and chop wood. They have given me my taste for intimacy and conversation, and less charming things: a willingness to be led on, to fantasise about scenes that I do not necessarily want to come true, an assumption that someone will mostly be there to listen. To the talk-show host interested in how to keep people reading, I could honestly have said, *I owe fiction all of that.* But when it comes to endings, I am on the side of real people, blood in our veins, lives rich with the possibilities that characters almost never get: of friendship, of staying happy, of starting all over again.

ACKNOWLEDGEMENTS

I am so grateful to the people who kept this manuscript going at all its stages: Alastair, Bruce, Christina, Chantal, David, David, Elizabeth, Kirsten, Michael, Sarah. This book is better for your intelligence, your criticism, your friendship.

Heiko, your curiosity and generosity are on most of these pages. Thank you for the stories.

Maibritt, I stole your bibliography format – forgive me, and come back and see us often.

Perry, you are a wizard and a strong-armed warrior: @goperry1!

Heather, I am still grateful for everything, every day.

Louisa Dunnigan, it's been a pleasure to realise what a good editor can do. You saw this project through from the very beginning with care and wisdom. All of the mistakes are mine, but you saved me from many others.

And to Eleanor Birne for representing the book and reading it at just the right moment.

READING LIST (CHRONOLOGICAL)

Madame de Lafayette, *The Princesse de Clèves* (France, 1678)

This is the novel that Nikolas Sarkozy singled out for criticism before he became president of France, claiming it was ridiculous that French students should be expected to answer questions about the novel in their Civil Service exams. As a result, public readings of the novel proliferated in the late 2000s.

Daniel Defoe, *Robinson Crusoe* (England, 1719)

There is a magazine story from the 1790s called 'Tales of a Robinson Crusoe' in which a much-loved edition of this novel becomes the narrator of its own demise, explaining how it has been given up by a young reader more disposed to magazines. Which only goes to show that the concern that novels are going out of fashion is as old as novels themselves.

Samuel Richardson, *Pamela* (England, 1740)

This was the first novel ever to produce fans: readers who wanted to know Pamela, to be like her, to wear her dresses and have pictures of her on their plates and their walls. Like all media hits, it also had its spin-offs and its detractors, and the success of *Pamela* was followed quite quickly by many satires of Pamela's adventures in sex and upward mobility.

Henry Fielding, *Amelia* (England, 1751)

I'm not exactly recommending this one – it has none of the swagger and structure of Fielding's more famous novel, *Tom Jones*. But it does map with wonderful verve the messy feel of life in metropolitan England in the eighteenth century. As London magistrate, and sponsor of the city's first full-time police force, Fielding knew what he was talking about.

Laurence Sterne, *The Life and Opinions of Tristram Shandy, Gentleman* (England, 1759–67)

The novel I once found so confusing that I wrote my PhD thesis about it. Now I find it so funny that I can't believe I used to miss all the jokes. If you think Sterne might be writing about sex, he certainly is. If you find it hard to read, try an audiobook – I suspect it's always been best enjoyed aloud.

Jean-Jacques Rousseau, *Julie; or, the New Eloise* (France, 1761)

As much a vehicle for Rousseau's radical critique of society as a novel for its own sake, *Julie* rails against doing what one should, in favour of doing what one genuinely feels to be right. It was this cause that Rousseau pursued his whole life, particularly in his philosophy of education.

Johan Wolfgang von Goethe, *The Sorrows of Young Werther* (Germany, 1774)

This novel, written in just five weeks, launched Goethe's literary career. It is famous partly for making it fashionable to commit suicide, with young men reconstructing the scene of Werther's death and leaving the novel to be found along with their own bodies. This never seemed quite credible to me, but it's a good story about the power of flash fiction.

Mary Wollstonecraft, *Mary: A Fiction* (England, 1788)

Wollstonecraft at her weakest is still very good to read. Angry, passionate on behalf of women, but not obviously their ally, she writes with an obstinacy and contrariness that I recognise. Her female characters bristle like friends I have fought with.

Jane Austen, *Pride and Prejudice* (England, 1813)

The genre of girl-meets-boy story is born here, along with the idea that the girl might reform that boy to make him someone she wants to marry.

Charlotte Brontë, *Jane Eyre* (England, 1847)

A duck–rabbit of a novel, to be read once as the story of a child wronged and neglected, and then at least one more time from the perspective of an adult who knows more about the world and can see that child within it.

Charlotte Brontë, *Villette* (England, 1853)

Although less generally celebrated than *Jane Eyre*, the gothic qualities of this novel, where the worlds of Lucy's mind and of the small town in Belgium are so unashamedly dark, have made it the favourite of some famous readers. Virginia Woolf found *Villette* admirable in its assertion 'I love. I hate. I suffer.'

Gustave Flaubert, *Madame Bovary* (France, 1857)

This was on the reading list for the university course I was taking on the novel when New York's Twin Towers fell in 2001. It was taught to me by the teacher I adored, who made us focus for hours on one scene where Emma and Rodolphe first meet.

Leo Tolstoy, *Anne Karenina* (Russia, 1878)

Ballgowns, ice-skating, hunting, racecourses and railway tracks. It's an amazing feat that this novel of high-society family life is so wonderful, its humanism so poignant, while its people are individually so spoiled.

George Gissing, *New Grub Street* (England, 1891)

I wish Marian had been the star of this novel, not just the amanuensis with inky fingers, too poor to marry in the end. I have often thought of her heroically, particularly on long days I spent in the old Reading Room of the British Library.

Reading List (Chronological)

Thomas Hardy, *Jude the Obscure* (England, 1895)

My mother says that what she likes in Hardy is that you can learn about how they used to do things in the past. I understand what she means, but *Jude* is one of the most forward-looking novels I know. Hardy is so impatient for the twentieth century to arrive and save his characters from their own moment.

Henry James, *What Maisie Knew* (USA, 1897)

This is one of the first novels ever to represent the effects of divorce on a child. James was helping to pull down the façades of Victorian England, but one senses that he himself regrets what he finds behind them. The novel is written in the third person, but is carefully focused through Maisie.

D. H. Lawrence, *Sons and Lovers* (England, 1913)

Many of the domestic scenes from my childhood are mixed in my head with scenes from this novel – of Paul burning the bread, or Mr Morrell washing by the fire. It delivered me imaginatively into the experience of being in a male body, in a way that many fictions must have delivered me into being in a woman's.

E. M. Forster, *Maurice* (England, 1914/1971)

Forster wrote this novel in 1914, but it was not published until after his death in 1970. His own verdict was that the novel was publishable, but that it would come at a high cost. In 1960 Forster wrote: 'Since *Maurice* was written there has been a change in the public attitude here: the change from ignorance and terror to familiarity and contempt.'

Ford Madox Ford, *The Good Soldier* (England, 1915)

The most famous scene in this novel involves Dowell laughing as he sees one cow throw another into a ditch, from the window of a train. The idea is that he doesn't see at all the violence underpinning the scene, but only the joke of it. Which is typical of Dowell's failure as a narrator – supposedly attentive, but always missing the darkness until it enfolds him.

Thomas Mann, *The Magic Mountain* (Germany, 1924)

This whole novel is often read as a meditation on time and whether tempo can itself be represented. In one scene Castorp finds himself sheltering from a blizzard that seems to last for hours, only to discover that his period of disaster has lasted merely a few minutes.

Willa Cather, *The Professor's House* (USA, 1925)

After a lifetime at the university, Godfrey St Peter is able to move his family into a new house. Disillusioned and increasingly bitter, he stays behind musing in his old study. As he withdraws further and further from life, his thoughts turn to the western adventures of the young engineer, Tom Outland.

Virginia Woolf, *Mrs Dalloway* (England, 1925)

I have eaten vegetables cultivated in an allotment very close to the garden house where Woolf wrote, and to the river where she drowned. Whenever I think of Clarissa I want to connect the well-tended fertility of that soil to the way ideas seem to bloom in Woolf's hand from her head.

D. H. Lawrence, *Lady Chatterley's Lover* (1928 – first published in Italy)

There's a famous scene where Mellors hangs oak-sprays and bluebells around Connie's breasts, sticks a pink campion flower in her belly button and weaves forget-me-nots into her pubic hair. If the mingling of bodies doesn't appeal, the botany might.

Laura Ingalls Wilder, *Little House on the Prairie Series* (USA, 1932–43)

Reading these books can feel like learning how to build a well, or a house in the bank of a river, or how to make pancakes without eggs. I read and reread them and still don't know how to do those things. Christmas always comes in Wilder's world, bringing pared-down, precious gifts.

Carson McCullers, *The Member of the Wedding* (USA, 1946)

McCullers came, like Shannon, from the American South to New York. It was there that she studied writing at NYU, leading to her success as a novelist, which helped to offset both her stormy marriage and her unrequited passion for several women she fell in love with, later in her life.

Patricia Highsmith, *The Price of Salt* (USA, 1952)

Highsmith reports having started this story after her encounter with a real Carol Aird, rich and blonde and dressed in mink. In the novel Carol invites Therese to her house and offers her a glass of milk that is warm and *saltless as chalk yet alive as a growing embryo.*

Boris Pasternak, *Doctor Zhivago* (Russia, 1957 – first published in Italy)

This novel wasn't published in the Soviet Union until 1987. On the face of things, the message is that Yuri Zhivago, the doctor-poet-philosopher, is crushed by his experience of the Russian Revolution. But the fine details of his experience throughout it also suggest all the ways in which poetry is made by it.

Muriel Spark, *The Prime of Miss Jean Brodie* (Scotland, 1961)

Come for the slice of Edinburgh history, stay for the sense of queer possibility and the strange sex appeal of Mr Lloyd, the golden-haired, one-armed art teacher at Blaine School, whose pictures all look like Miss Brodie.

James Baldwin, *Another Country* (USA, 1962)

Sex, suicide, poverty, ambition, racism, anger, exile: as this group of friends crosses Manhattan, Baldwin's topic is always love. The novel branches out into the world, with some of its chapters set in France, but loops back to America in a swerve of optimism.

Doris Lessing, *The Golden Notebook* (England, 1962)

The first lines of this novel, which concern the interaction between women, turn out at the end to have been gifted to

Anna by her lover, Saul. This gives the whole novel a bewildering circularity, suggesting that the scenes on which it seems to report in real time can obviously only have been written after the fact.

Mary McCarthy, *The Group* (USA, 1963)

The topic here seems to be love, but in fact these women are bound together by almost anything but that. Their Manhattan is an earlier, pettier one than Baldwin's, and suicide is less likely to lead to redemption.

Ursula K. Le Guin, *A Wizard of Earthsea* (USA, 1968)

Ged, the arrogant, impatient, impetuous wizard boy, eventually becomes the wisest of them all. This is the story of his lonely rise to power in a world where he travels among worthy fellows.

Margaret Drabble, *The Waterfall* (England, 1969)

All the days pass slowly in this novel, but the longest ones are when Jane is alone with her children, who are also very much present in all the scenes of the novel. In contrast to many later fictions about parenting and family life, Drabble's handling of children centres on that relation of caretaking with minimal preciousness.

James Salter, *Light Years* (USA, 1975)

Nedra shops in Zabar's in Manhattan; Viri has his shirts hand-made and monogrammed. These details have stuck with me as importantly luxurious, objectionably decadent, but also central to the pleasure of this novel, which lies very largely in sumptuous sentences describing fine but also somehow ordinary things.

Helen Garner, *Monkey Grip* (Australia, 1977)

I got to love this novel again while writing this book, having remembered it all my life simply as a magic opening onto my parents' alternative life in an Australian city. It is in fact a classic, with whole parts of inner-city Melbourne still recognisable to readers as places that feature in the novel.

Penelope Fitzgerald, *Offshore* (England, 1979)

I think of Nenna, the young single mother in this Booker Prize-winning novel, looking like my mother when she was in her early thirties: short hair, short shorts. The last section of the story describes an evening when Nenna has sex with two different men that she loves, but the shock-value of this is deeply buried within Fitzgerald's wonderful economy of prose.

Elizabeth Hardwick, *Sleepless Nights* (USA, 1979)

Having written all these pages in tribute to this novel, I can only say it should be read by everyone. But it's also worth noting that Hardwick's perspective, as a girl from Kentucky who ended up being very rich in New York, doesn't always stretch to the people who iron her clothes or make her dinner.

Reading List (Chronological)

Alan Hollinghurst, *The Swimming Pool Library* (England, 1988)

This is set partly in the Russell Hotel, which is very close to the hospital where Shannon was treated in London, which is close to Gay's the Word bookshop, where I bought my first copy of it. I feel somehow knitted into the spaces of this book, even though I am in other ways no part of its story.

Jeanette Winterson, *Written on the Body* (England, 1992)

The internet tells me Winterson is married now, so I guess she changed her mind about some things. I find it brave to have a narrator who defies gender.

Ali Smith, *The Accidental* (England, 2005)

I have tried to write analytically about this novel in the past, but the character of Amber, the stranger who arrives at the family house, throws me. Her presence is a tribute to Pasolini's *Theorem*, but she's also a film itself, walking around inside a novel.

Karl Ove Knausgård, *My Struggle* (Norway, 2009–11)

A lot of people talk about this as a universal story of parenting and creating. I feel as if it's actually a very Scandinavian story. You need a lot of parental leave in order to write this way about the pressures of parenting.

Elena Ferrante, *Neapolitan Quartet* (Italy, 2012–15)

I read these novels while Hans and I lived in a tiny flat in

North London with the kids. A story never felt so like a place into which one could disappear. Italian friends tell me that Ferrante's identity was never actually a mystery.

André Alexis, *Fifteen Dogs* (Canada, 2015)

Gifted by the gods with language and consciousness, fifteen dogs in Toronto go different ways. Prince, who becomes a poet, is the one who seems to prove that human abilities can be the cause of happiness, but he is also terribly alone at the end of the novel.

Sally Rooney, *Conversations with Friends* (Ireland, 2017)

I taught this one online during the pandemic. I was thinking the Danish students would simply enjoy the read, but in fact they objected firmly to its stigmatisation of S&M: why, they asked, was this something you'd only be interested in when feeling abject and depressed?

Lisa Halliday, *Asymmetry* (USA, 2018)

Drawing on her relationship as a young editor with Philip Roth, Halliday has made the most of having to write under the influence of an older writer. But this novel is also about it being perfectly okay to make things up, so it would be wrong to judge it too much by the biographies involved.

Tayari Jones, *An American Marriage* (USA, 2018)

This novel has the quality of a modern *Odyssey* – time is passing as the married couple fight huge obstacles that keep him in prison and prevent them growing old together.

Reading List (Chronological)

Ocean Vuong, *On Earth We're Briefly Gorgeous* (USA, 2019)

Marie thinks this book contains the saddest sentence ever written. It describes a child's cheap trainers flashing like the *smallest ambulances in the world.*

REFERENCES

Love and the Novel draws in different ways on the following non-fictional texts. I am very grateful for all of them. They are listed here in their original editions.

Hannah Arendt, *The Human Condition* (University of Chicago Press, 1958).

Nancy Armstrong, *Desire and Domestic Fiction: A Political History of the Novel* (Oxford University Press, 1987).

James Baldwin, *The Fire Next Time* (Dial Press, 1963).

Roland Barthes, *A Lover's Discourse: Fragments*, trans. Richard Howard (Hill and Wang, 1979; first published in French in 1977).

Simone de Beauvoir, *The Second Sex*, trans. Constance Borde and Sheila Malovany-Chevallier (Knopf, 2009; first published in French in 1949).

——*Letters to Sartre*, ed. and trans. Quintin Hoare (Arcade, 1990; first published in French in 1990).

Boston Women's Health Book Collective, *Women and Their Bodies* (later *Our Bodies, Ourselves*) (1970, New England Free Press).

Pierre Bourdieu, *Distinction: A Social Critique of the*

Judgement of Taste, trans. Richard Nice (Harvard University Press, 1984; first published in French in 1979).

Carol Brightman (ed.), *Between Friends: The Correspondence of Hannah Arendt and Mary McCarthy, 1949–1975* (Harcourt Brace, 1995).

Suzanne Brøgger, *Deliver Us from Love: A Radical Feminist Speaks Out* (Delacorte Press, 1976).

Edmund Burke, *Reflections on the Revolution in France* (James Dodsley, 1790).

Judith Butler, *Gender Trouble: Feminism and the Subversion of Identity* (Routledge, 1999).

Terry Castle, *The Professor and Other Writings* (HarperCollins, 2010).

Stefan Collini, *Common Reading: Critics, Historians, Publics* (Oxford University Press, 2009).

Alex Comfort, *The Joy of Sex* (Crown, 1972).

Mark Currie, *About Time: Narrative, Fiction and the Philosophy of Time* (Edinburgh University Press, 2007).

Carolyn Dinshaw, *How Soon Is Now: Medieval Texts, Amateur Readers, and the Queerness of Time* (Duke University Press, 2010).

Geoff Dyer, *Out of Sheer Rage: Wrestling with D. H. Lawrence* (Picador, 2009).

Lee Edelman, *No Future: Queer Theory and the Death Drive* (Duke University Press, 2004).

Friedrich Engels, *The Origin of the Family, Private Property and the State* (first published in German in 1884).

Elzbieta Ettinger, *Hannah Arendt and Martin Heidegger* (Yale University Press, 1997).

Mary Favret, *War at a Distance: Romanticism and the*

Making of Modern Wartime (Princeton University Press, 2010).

Michel Foucault, *The History of Sexuality, Vol. 1*, trans. Robert Hurley (Pantheon, 1978; first published in French in 1976).

——'Friendship as a Way of Life' in *The Essential Works of Michael Foucault, 1954–1984, Vol. 1: Ethics*, trans. Robert Hurley et al., ed. Paul Rabinow (The New Press, 1997).

Silvia Frederici, *Revolution at Point Zero: Housework, Reproduction, and Feminist Struggle* (PM Press, 2020).

Elizabeth Freeman, *Time Binds: Queer Temporalities, Queer Histories* (Duke University Press, 2010).

Nancy Friday, *My Secret Garden: Women's Sexual Fantasies* (Trident Press, 1973).

William Galperin, *The Historical Austen* (University of Pennsylvania Press, 2005).

Helen Garner, *Everywhere I Look* (Text Publishing Company, 2016).

William Godwin, *An Enquiry Concerning Political Justice and Its Influence on Moral and Happiness* (1793).

Germaine Greer, *The Female Eunuch* (MacGibbon and Kee, 1970).

Lauren Jae Gutterman, *Her Neighbor's Wife: A History of Lesbian Desire Within Marriage* (University of Pennsylvania Press, 2019).

Saskia Hamilton (ed.), *The Dolphin Letters, 1970–79: Elizabeth Hardwick, Robert Lowell, and Their Circle* (Farrar, Straus and Giroux, 2019).

Amber Hollibaugh, *My Dangerous Desires: A Queer Girl Dreaming Her Way Home* (Duke University Press, 2000).

Annemarie Jagose, *Orgasmology* (Duke University Press, 2012).

Claire Jarvis, *Exquisite Masochism: Marriage, Sex, and the Novel Form* (Johns Hopkins University Press, 2016).

Myra Jehlen, *Five Fictions in Search of Truth* (Princeton University Press, 2008).

Jonathan Kramnick, *Paper Minds: Literature and the Ecology of Consciousness* (University of Chicago Press, 2018).

Hermione Lee, *Penelope Fitzgerald: A Life Biography* (Vintage, 2015).

Caroline Levine, *Forms: Whole, Rhythm, Hierarchy, Network* (Princeton University Press, 2015).

Deborah Levy, *Tough Enough: Arbus, Arendt, Didion, McCarthy, Sontag, Weil* (University of Chicago Press, 2017).

Alison Light, *Radical Romance: A Memoir of Life, Love, and Consolation* (Fig Tree, 2019).

Audre Lorde, *A Burst of Light* (Firebrand Books, 1988).

Heather Love, *Underdogs: Social Deviance and Queer Theory* (Chicago University Press, 2021).

Niklas Luhmann, *Love as Passion: The Codification of Intimacy*, trans. Jeremy Gaines and Doris L. Jones (Stanford University Press, 1998; first published in German in 1982).

Deidre Lynch, *Loving Literature: A Cultural History* (University of Chicago Press, 2015).

Robin McCoy, *Late Bloomers: Awakening to Lesbianism After Forty* (Writers Club Press, 2000).

Michael McKeon, *The Secret History of Domesticity: Public,*

Private, and the Division of Knowledge (Johns Hopkins University Press, 2006).

Alberto Manguel, *A History of Reading* (Penguin, 1997).

Sharon Marcus, *Between Women: Friendship, Desire, and Marriage in Victorian England* (Princeton University Press, 2007).

Andrew Miller, *The Burdens of Perfection: On Ethics and Reading in Nineteenth-Century British Literature* (Cornell University Press, 2008).

D. A. Miller, *Jane Austen, Or, The Secret of Style* (Princeton University Press, 2003).

Kate Millett, *Sexual Politics: A Surprising Examination of Society's Most Arbitrary Folly* (Doubleday, 1970).

John Mullan, *Sentiment and Sociability: The Language of Feeling in the Eighteenth Century* (Clarendon Press, 1988).

José Esteban Muñoz, *Cruising Utopia: The Then and There of Queer Futurity* (NYU Press, 1999).

Maggie Nelson, *The Argonauts* (Graywolf Press, 2016).

Martha Nussbaum, *Love's Knowledge: Essays on Love and Literature* (Oxford University Press, 1990).

Nena O'Neill and George O'Neill, *Open Marriage: A New Life Style for Couples* (M. Evans and Co., 1972).

Ruth Perry, *Novel Relations: The Transformation of Kinship in English Literature and Culture, 1748–1818* (Cambridge University Press, 2004).

Adam Phillips, *Monogamy* (Vintage, 1999).

Mark Philp, *Reforming Ideas in Britain: Politics and Language in the Shadow of the French Revolution, 1789–1815* (Cambridge University Press, 2013).

Adela Pinch, *Thinking About Other People in Nineteenth-Century British Writing* (Cambridge, 2010).

Leah Price, *What We Talk About When We Talk About Books* (Basic Books, 2019).

Sophie Ratcliffe, *The Lost Properties of Love: An Exhibition of Myself* (William Collins, 2019).

Bruce Robbins, *The Servant's Hand: Fiction from Below* (Duke University Press, 1993).

Gillian Rose, *Love's Work: A Reckoning with Life* (Schocken Books, 1995).

Matthew Rubery, *The Untold Story of the Talking Book* (Harvard University Press, 2016).

Martin Ryle and Kate Soper, *To Relish the Sublime: Culture and Self-Realization in Postmodern Times* (Verso, 2002).

Elaine Scarry, *On Beauty and Being Just* (Princeton University Press, 1999).

Eve Kosofsky Sedgwick, *A Dialogue on Love* (Beacon Press, 1999).

Carolyn Steedman, *Landscape for a Good Woman: A Story of Two Lives* (Rutgers University Press, 1987).

Lawrence Stone, *The Family, Sex and Marriage in England, 1500–1800* (Harper, 1983).

Tony Tanner, *Adultery and the Novel: Contract and Transgression* (Johns Hopkins University Press, 1979).

Janet Todd, *Mary Wollstonecraft: A Revolutionary Life* (Columbia University Press, 2000).

Michael Warner, *The Trouble with Normal: Sex, Politics, and the Ethics of Queer Life* (The Free Press, 1999).

Ian Watt, *The Rise of the Novel* (University of California Press, 1974).

Gillian White, *Lyric Shame: The 'Lyric' Subject of*

Contemporary American Poetry (Harvard University Press, 2014).

Mary Wollstonecraft, *A Vindication of the Rights of Women: with Strictures on Political and Moral Subjects* (1792).

——*Letters Written During a Short Residence in Sweden, Norway, and Denmark* (1796).

Alex Woloch, *The One vs. the Many: Minor Characters and the Space of the Protagonist in the Novel* (Princeton University Press, 2004).